The Spiritual Work
of Marriage

The Spiritual Work
of Marriage

David C. Olsen

Routledge
Taylor & Francis Group

Routledge
Taylor & Francis Group
270 Madison Avenue
New York, NY 10016

Routledge
Taylor & Francis Group
2 Park Square
Milton Park, Abingdon
Oxon OX14 4RN

Visit the Taylor & Francis Web site at
http://www.taylorandfrancis.com

and the Routledge Web site at
http://www.routledge.com

ABOUT THE AUTHOR

David Olsen, MS, MSW, PhD, has served as executive director of Samaritan Counseling Center since its inception in 1985. He is also an adjunct professor at Sage Graduate School, where he teaches couples therapy and sex therapy. He is a certified pastoral counselor and is a certified marriage and family therapist, a licensed clinical social worker, and Diplomate in the American Board of Examiners in Clinical Social Work. He is an ordained minister in the American Baptist Churches, USA. He holds an MS in counseling from Oneonta State University College, and an MSW from the University at Albany, and a master's degree and a PhD in psychology from Drew University. Dr. Olsen has done extensive postgraduate work in family therapy. He is author of *Integrative Family Therapy;* he co-authored *The Couples Survival Workbook, When Helping Starts to Hurt,* and *When Helping Starts to Hurt: A New Look At Burnout Among Psychotherapists* (1994), and a chapter in *Prevention: Avoiding Burnout in a Perilous Calling.* Dr. Olsen has also published numerous journal articles and is a regular contributor to local media articles and features.

CONTENTS

Chapter 1

Introduction

Therefore a man leaves his father and his mother and clings to his wife, and they became one flesh. And the man and his wife were both naked, and were not ashamed.

Genesis 2:24, 25 (NIV)

THE DREAM

The candles had all been lit, the bride looked lovely in her wedding gown, and the groom smiled as he turned to face her and took her hands in his to repeat their vows. Despite shaky voices, they ended their vows confidently with the words "'til death do us part." They looked at that moment like the perfect couple. The photographer tried to capture the moment. Their families smiled, shed some tears, and prayed for a happy marriage. The reception that followed was grand. People danced and partied and celebrated the beginning of this couple's life together. Everything looked perfect. It was the culmination of a year of planning and what appeared to be a storybook romance beginning in their last year of college. Their future could not have looked brighter for this couple; both had secure and exciting jobs and the possibilities looked limitless.

In preparation for this day, they had been through a number of sessions of premarital counseling required by their minister, and even tried to take it seriously. However, in all honesty they could not really anticipate any long-term problems. They ended their premarital counseling convinced that there was no problem that they could not solve. They discussed money, in-laws, careers, roles, religion, and were

convinced that they were going to have a wonderful married life together. They sincerely believed that their love in the end would con-
quer any problems that emerged between them.

The religious wedding service that consecrated their vows invoked
the magic and sacredness of marriage. Vows are made before God;
religious language and religious symbols are utilized. "What God has
joined together, let no man put asunder" is a statement often used as
part of the vows. Scripture readings are utilized, and prayers are em-
ployed to bless the union of husband and wife. Although the symbols
and rituals vary in different religious traditions, all the traditions im-
ply that marriage is a spiritual union. Implied within this, although
frequently not understood, is that there is a powerful spiritual dimension to marriage and that marriage can be a vehicle for spiritual work.

Paul Stookey (of Peter, Paul, and Mary) in "The Wedding Song,"
summarized it as follows:

> The union of your spirits here has caused Him to remain,
> For whenever two or more of you are gathered in His name,
> there is love.

We have all witnessed some variation of this wedding scene whether
at our own wedding or the wedding of family and friends. We watch the
beauty of the service unfold, and experience a wide range of emotions.
We are occasionally in touch with the spiritual mystery of the moment,
and hope and pray that the couple will find lasting joy and happiness.

THE REALITY

Despite premarital counseling, a wonderful wedding, spiritual ritual, and supportive families, the odds of this couple having a happy
marriage are statistically not in their favor. The odds are 50-50 that
they will even stay married. The odds are even more depressing that
they will find long-term happiness and deep marital satisfaction. Finding lasting marital bliss is elusive for most couples.

The late psychiatrist and author, M. Scott Peck (2003), began his
best seller *The Road Less Traveled,* with the classic line, "Life is difficult." What an understatement! The reality is that life is often one problem after another. If life is hard, then marriage is even more difficult,

and unfortunately, statistics support this. Despite the best planning, premarital counseling, and wonderful weddings, good long-term marriages are rare. Approximately 50 percent of first marriages fail, and of the other half that make it, it is not clear how many are actually satisfying marriages.

"For those who try it a second time or third time, the statistics get worse instead of better; approximately 60 percent of remarriages fail" (http://www.smartmarriages.com/remarrying.html). In other words, very few people learn from their mistakes and do better the next time around in a new relationship. The reality is that while M. Scott Peck's words are true—life is hard, it is even more of a reality that marriage is difficult, and that the odds of achieving a great marriage are not good. The reality is that most couples do not find the marital satisfaction that they are seeking. Despite the spiritual rituals involved in the wedding, marriage for most does not become a place for spiritual growth and work.

In light of these realities it is not surprising that there is no shortage of literature on marriage that aims at helping couples remedy these problems and find the satisfaction that they are seeking. Numerous books have been written for couples that focus on helping them in a variety of ways such as learning better communication skills and shifting counterproductive communication patterns, learning tools for working through conflict, understanding and resolving underlying belief systems about marriage and about their partner, resolving the issues from the families we grew up in, as well as books on how best to understand and shift the conscious and unconscious marital contracts between couples. There is no shortage of books, articles, tapes, and DVDs. Browse the self-help section of any major bookstore and you will be overwhelmed by the amount of books dedicated to this topic. As if that were not enough, most popular magazines have a column on how to improve marital satisfaction in a variety of ways ranging from ways to improve sex to negotiating ways to fight fair.

Despite the amazing amount of literature designed to help people improve their marriages, there is very little that even acknowledges that there is a profound spiritual dimension to it, much less provides guidance on how to conduct oneself in this realm.

Even in the world of the church, marriage as spiritual work is rarely talked about. Despite the religious symbols, words, and vows that were used during the wedding, there is very little written about the spiritual work of marriage. Sadly, this idea is not even introduced. Who talks about this? How many couples actually talk about the spiritual work involved in marriage? In fact, quite often, couples are ashamed to reveal to their religious communities that they even have marital problems and are ashamed to admit they are in therapy. The notion of the spiritual work of marriage is not discussed.

To even begin to think of marriage as a spiritual journey, we need to acknowledge its difficulty at the beginning. The First Noble Truth of Buddhism is that there is suffering in life (a la Scott Peck), and subsequent teachings talk about how to work with it. The reason for beginning with this truth is to normalize the reality that all humans experience pain and challenges. We can then let go of any stigma of "failure" when we experience struggles, and it is thus easier to learn tools to work with them. The Judeo-Christian tradition speaks to the same issue. The first mythical marriage, Adam and Eve, goes bad quickly. Starting in an idyllic garden setting, it quickly degenerates to blame, accusation, shame, and separation. Suffering enters the first marriage quickly and most of the scriptures focus on the redemption of that suffering and separation.

However, although Adam and Eve could be seen as the original troubled married, most couples do not heed their example and are not prepared for its suffering, or separation, when idealization gets lost. As a result they miss an opportunity for profound spiritual work.

Unfortunately, in modern culture, the wedding itself is seen as a fruition, a dream come true. The challenge of marriage as a path to open oneself up to another and love and forgive and heal does not seem to be a part of the ceremony, or it may be given lip service; however, then the couple is left on their own. After the excitement and joy of the wedding, what help is given to couples to begin the journey of the spiritual work of marriage? Unfortunately, very little help is provided.

SPIRITUALITY VERSUS RELIGION

Part of understanding the spiritual work of marriage is beginning to understand the difference between spirituality and religion especially as it pertains to relationships. Religion is the institutionalized form of spirituality. Religion is typically focused on an organized belief system, shared moral values, and a faith community or organization to be committed to. Religion can provide a shared ideology (way of looking at the world). The great psychoanalyst Erik Erikson points out that this ideology helps organize and bolster a strong sense of identity. Knowing what you believe about the world and being with others who believe the same thing gives a strong sense of who you are, and thus reduces anxiety many feel without such support. Many couples and families find both a deep sense of grounding as well as a sense of identity that is supported by formal religious participation. Life cycle events in families are quite often celebrations within religious traditions. For example, in some Christian religious traditions, the beginning of life is celebrated through baptism of the infant; catechisms and confirmations mark a rite of passage for children; weddings become a spiritual celebration of marriage, and funerals mark the end of life. In a similar way, Judaism provides for the family observance of rituals such as the weekly Shabbat (Sabbath), celebrating of major holidays in the Jewish calendar year, and rituals across the life cycle (Walsh, 2003).

For many couples and families their religious involvement and participation in their faith community is a central part of their family life, so it should not be surprising to suggest to couples that they consider the spiritual aspect of marriage. Yet religion and spirituality are not necessarily equivalent. Religion helps bolster identity, and thus lowers anxiety. However, the spiritual journey can be very threatening to one's sense of self. Having to forgive, be vulnerable in spite of shame all increase anxiety and can be frightening. Marriage is not for the faint of heart. Unlike religious ideology, which reduces anxiety by providing a clear view of the world and of what to believe, the spiritual journey of marriage is anxiety producing for many reasons. No wonder the spiritual work of marriage gets so little attention.

SPIRITUALITY

Many writers distinguish spirituality from religion. While religion is focused on shared belief and a faith community, spirituality can be thought of differently. It can be seen as part of organized religion, or can stand apart from it. The late theologian Paul Tillich (1951, 2000) spoke of spirituality as finding connection to the "ground of all being." Spirituality is a very personal experience. It has to do with a deep sense of values and a way of being in the world. It can be compatible with religious affiliation, a set of morals, or a sense of belief. For many people today, there is a suspicion of organized religion. Accompanying this rejection of ideology, there remains a longing for a deeply felt spirituality that is lived.

Spiritual seekers often begin their journey after some personal crisis—death of a loved one, existential crisis or search for meaning, serious illness, etc. (Again life is hard.) Spirituality seems to be motivated by a need to understand the self in relation to the unknown, the universe, God. It is a need to understand it beyond the confines of religious institutions. It is a very personal journey that is often solitary, but it can also be part of a couple's journey together. In fact, couples can even experience a spiritual intimacy. This can be one of the most fulfilling aspects of one's marriage that can occur as a couple takes on this journey together.

MARRIAGE AND SPIRITUALITY

For many couples, both organized religion and some sense of spirituality are an important part of their lives. Usually, the wedding that begins their life together is grounded in some type of religious ceremony. If children become part of their lives, then they look to their religious institutions for a ritual such as baptism and some sort of catechism or faith formation to help ground their children in the religious tradition. At the end of the life cycle, religious funerals complete the journey of life and provide meaning, hope, and comfort. So on some level, the religious couple is grounded in religious observance that mark and celebrate the major life cycle events. Often these life cycle events involve the extended family at a baptism, wedding, or funeral, so not only is the couple grounded in their religious heritage but also the larger family system is as well. All of these religious rituals calm anxiety around these transitions of life and death.

Although these rituals and life cycle events are important and can be helpful, they do not in themselves address the spiritual work of marriage. In the journey of marriage there is conflict, hurt, misunderstanding, tragedy, joy, disappointment, just to name a few. Here, the couple is alone facing pain themselves without the calming force of religion. The spiritual work is the need to mature—to face one's own existential anxiety and come to an understanding and mature response to life and death. There are opportunities for growth, opportunities to learn more about oneself and one's partner. In reality, these struggles can be wonderful opportunities to do spiritual work. If marriage begins with a sacred religious ceremony, then the work of marriage is fundamentally spiritual. Unfortunately, most newlyweds miss this message or are not ready for it in the first place. Genuine spiritual growth happens when one is pushed to grow and unfortunately much of this growth results from pain.

Most Christian religious traditions have a language that is part of faith formation. Words and concepts are used to help express the truths of their religion. Words such as idolatry, grace and acceptance, repentance, and forgiveness are common terms in most religious traditions. During times of religious instruction these terms are defined and explained as aspects of religious ideology, and on a good day many people could at least give a decent explanation of these spiritual concepts that is intellectually coherent. Living out these concepts is a different story and is far from easy. Perhaps that is part of the skepticism about organized religion. Many would say that "followers" should spend more time living out their faith and less time talking about it.

LIVED SPIRITUALITY

The essence of a spiritual life is not the ability to understand, define, and explain certain key propositions of the religious ideology. Spirituality in the end is a way of truly living out what you say you believe so that it is woven into the fabric of life. It is what some preachers have referred to as "walking the talk." It is not about what you say you believe, it is much more about how what you believe is woven into the fabric of life and relationship.

Words like idolatry, grace, acceptance, repentance, and forgiveness are important words with deep spiritual and theological meaning, in the end they are words that must be lived. It is one thing to define forgiveness and be able to understand what it means; it is quite another thing to practice forgiving once you have been hurt by someone you care about. It is one thing to talk about repentance or to pray the prayer of confession as part of a religious liturgy; however, it is quite another to actually admit you are wrong, offer to change, and actually practice "repentance" within the context of a committed relationship.

It is one thing to talk about grace and acceptance as a concept. It is a whole different issue to try to be accepting of someone who down deep you really wish would change. Embodying all of these often form the challenges of marriage. We grow into it.

MARRIAGE AS SPIRITUAL CRUCIBLE

In the end, marriage is a type of spiritual crucible. The couple who celebrate the joy of their marriage witnessed by family and friends will hopefully have a wonderful wedding album to celebrate the event. Hopefully, they will always cherish the day they were married and see it as magical. However, realistically they are entering a spiritual crucible that will challenge them to live out their spirituality with each other.

On the day of their wedding they gazed deeply into each other's eyes as they recited their vows and anticipated a joy filled life together. The bride had never looked so beautiful to her soon-to-be husband, and she looked at him with deep love and respect. They felt a love that ran deep, anticipated a relaxing honeymoon, and then a great life together. The moment seemed perfect, as if time had stopped.

Who would have predicted that three years later they were caught in an endless cycle of arguing and withdrawal? They were rapidly drifting into a parallel-track marriage focused on their respective careers. Idealization was turning to disillusionment. What once seemed perfect and sacred was feeling cold and distant.

THE SPIRITUAL OPPORTUNITY

For some couples this is the beginning of the end. If they continue down the slope of disillusionment, they will find themselves more and more distant and bitter, and may easily become part of the 50 percent of couples who end up divorced. Sadly, many feel that they have failed and often feel like they have failed in the eyes of the church, or they can see this as a spiritual and relational opportunity. All marriages go through some level of disillusionment and distance; it is inevitable.

However, there is hope in the midst of crisis. For couples who are willing to work and see this is as spiritual opportunity, there is potential for wonderful marital growth and intimacy. In addition, there is an opportunity for deep spiritual growth; an opportunity to live out those spiritual concepts that have been talked about in religious communities.

This book is for those couples who want to engage in that challenge, who see their relationship as worth working on, and see it as an opportunity for spiritual work and growth. The chapters that follow will introduce several key spiritual concepts with practical ways of understanding these concepts within the profound journey of marriage. For those who practice these concepts, marriage can be a taste of heaven on earth and a possibility for deep spiritual work.

Chapter 2

The Longing to Be Known

Patients will talk about the need to be seen, known, responded to, confirmed, appreciated, cared for, mirrored. . . . The need for each individual to feel a sense of witnessed significance for his or her life has traditionally been noticed and responded to by religion.

Paul Fleischman, 1990, p. 7

O Lord, you have searched me and you know me. You know when I sit and when I rise; you perceive my thoughts from afar. . . . Before a word is on my tongue you know it completely.

Psalm 139:1, 2, 4 (NIV)

Debra sat down in her therapist's office and sighed deeply. Her eyes began to fill with tears. "I am just so lonely. I've been married more than twenty years and I am more lonely now than ever. Mark just doesn't get it. He doesn't know me. He means well, he tries, but we just are not connected. I am always left feeling like he just doesn't get who I am, or what I need from him, and when I try to describe what I am feeling, he always makes a joke that leaves me more misunderstood. How, after all these years, could this be? Am I so difficult to understand? He knows that I am dealing with aging parents who are very demanding, but he never seems to understand what I am going through. I'm not going to leave, but I can't go on like this. I just want him to get it."

Debra's complaint and description of loneliness describe the profound human longing to be understood. Perhaps nothing is as lonely as being married to someone who just doesn't get it. Most people, regardless of whether they can articulate it, long to be understood. The longing to be known is one of the most fundamental human desires.

BEING KNOWN AS A SPIRITUAL GOAL

The deep human desire to be known and to be seen is deeply spiritual. The Jewish philosopher Martin Buber (1996) spoke of it as the desire for an "I-Thou" relationship. This implies that within this deep human encounter, something spiritual or transcendent occurs. He contrasts an "I-Thou" relationship with an "I-It" relationship. The "I-It" relationship reduces the other person to a category, limiting the person within a narrow role such as husband or wife, or cold or emotional. Examples would be the husband who claims, "She is just always so emotional," which limits how she is seen, and blocks understanding. Or the wife who says "All he values is his work. He doesn't enjoy being with me." When people reduce their partners to these descriptions they see their partner as an "It" and deep understanding is not possible. In contrast, deep understanding occurs only when people are seen apart from narrow categories. This allows people to be seen as "Thou." At those moments something profoundly spiritual has occurred. These are the magic moments in marriage when you feel deeply understood and can feel your whole body relax. In those moments, it is as if you are seeing your partner in a whole different way and getting to know your partner in a deeper and more spiritual way. It is what people mean when they say "When you look at me that way, I just melt." When we feel this happening, we often call it "falling in love."

Fleischman (1990) says one of the universal religious truths found in all religions is the desire for "witnessed significance." This longing goes beyond the profound human desire to be seen and known by parents, and partners; it refers to the desire to be known on a spiritual level, as well as being known on a relational level. In psychoanalytic theory this is referred to as "empathic attunement," i.e., the ability of one person to deeply know the other, by being able to fully immerse oneself in the subjective world of the other. It is the experience of feeling like someone you care about really gets it, which usually results in a very positive feeling. Try and remember a time when you were depressed or anxious or agitated. You describe the feeling to your partner, and he or she "gets it" in a way that helps you feel totally understood. As you feel understood, you probably felt more relaxed and soothed, and may have even felt that relaxation in your body. Your problem was not solved, but you felt like the person you care about most really understood and was totally with you. That is empathy. That is the experience of being known. For most people it does not happen often enough.

Sam collapsed on the couch on a Saturday morning with his cup of coffee and the newspaper. His wife Irene was working in the kitchen. The tension between them was palpable. Sam finally broke the ice. "This feels terrible: I don't know why we keep having the same argument." Irene bit her lip, and did not say what she usually did about Sam never talking and being emotionally shut down. She tried to listen. To her surprise Sam continued, "I hate to keep hurting you—I want to be what you need, but it feels like I constantly hurt you." Irene responded quietly, "I know you don't want to hurt me—and I know you really love me." Sam softened more. He partially expected Irene to launch into one of her psychological theories about why he shut down. He wasn't sure what to do next. He tried to continue, "I think I get anxious about sharing too much of what I feel and I'm not sure why." Irene responded gently, "It's almost like you are afraid that I'll reject you if you share too many feelings—it's like you feel pressured to keep everything together all the time." She continued hesitantly, "and I'm afraid I reinforce that by being critical of you." Sam teared up briefly, and tried to pretend that something was in his eye. He hesitantly continued, "I don't know if this has anything to do with things, but my father would ridicule me if I ever expressed a feeling, and told me only girls cry. I could never do anything right in his eyes, and so I tried to always keep a low profile and share as little as possible." Irene now had tears in her eyes; she had never heard Sam talk like this before. She took a chance, sat on the couch with him and put her arm around him. She responded softly, "I'm sorry. It must be so hard to open up after feeling so put down growing up. I'm so glad you are telling me—I understand now how tough it is for you. I love you and want you to feel safe with me." With that Sam totally relaxed, put his head on his wife's shoulder and began to cry softly. All he could say was "thank you," and Irene wisely knew not to push further. Sam felt like she got it—that the person he loved really understood and wanted him to feel safe, and the relaxation in his body proved it.

KNOWING AND INCARNATION

This type of knowing is deeply spiritual and may be one of the ultimate expressions of spirituality and of love. In Christian theology, this deep type of knowing is described as incarnation, the belief that God entered human history in Jesus. Incarnation suggests that God entered our world and our reality by becoming one of us, and therefore was fully immersed in our experience. The ancient creeds of the early church described it as the experience of being fully God and fully man. Hebrews 4:15 (NIV) describes it like this, "For we do not have a high priest who is unable to sympathize with our weaknesses, but we have one who has been tempted in every way, just as we are—yet was without sin." In other words, this concept posits a God who understands us fully through the ultimate exercise of empathic attunement. God literally entered human experience, encountered suffering, pain, temptation, and loss; God understands deeply. On a spiritual level Irene was being "incarnational." She was able to not say what she usually said, and tried her best to enter her husband's subjective world.

Part of the spiritual work of marriage is to learn, like Irene, to be "incarnational" and deeply empathic in our relationships. That is, to develop the ability to move fully into the subjective world of our partner and to attempt to understand him or her as opposed to making assumptions. This is obviously very difficult work since most of the time we reactively see our partner through the filter of our assumptions.

To reverse this and really "see" involves letting go of our assumptions, and at times our own needs, in the interest of better understanding the essence of our partner. Think about what happens when we try. Usually, we see through the filters of our own assumptions, or get defensive, and in the end do not really get it. Often, I have heard couples practice careful listening skills and reflect back to the other the content of what they were saying, but still leaving the other feeling misunderstood.

This is one of the most difficult things to do in relationships. Unfortunately, most couples believe that they really know and understand each other, and that assumption actually makes their problems worse. These assumptions block their ability to "see" their partner. Phrases like "He knows what I need and refuses to give it to me" block connection. What if Irene had come to this conclusion? Instead of graciously trying to understand, she might have been angry and critical. Or if Sam assumed, "She knows how angry it makes me when she tries to get me to share," he would then logically be even more distant. These assumptions block the ability to empathically understand. In Buber's (1996) language they turn our partners into "Its" and block the "Thou" experience. One of the problems of marriage is that people act on the basis of their assumptions and beliefs without ever questioning if those beliefs are even true. Sadly, in doing this, we are closing our hearts to our partner. The spiritual experience of being in love, of having an "I-Thou" experience is clouded over by our assumptions and habitual responses. We probably also feel that our partner is doing the same to us.

If one of the most powerful human needs is the desire to be understood, why is this need so rarely met? Why is it so hard to give one's partner what they long for the most? Two things usually block our ability to do this. One is our own need to be understood and the ways we easily get defensive when we do not feel understood. The other is the assumptions and belief systems we form about our partner.

THE POWER OF BELIEF

Part of what interferes with the spiritual work of deep understanding and empathic attunement are the belief systems we hold; belief systems that at times we are not even aware of. Cognitive theory reminds us that we never hear in a "pure" way. Rather, we hear through the filters of our belief systems. Older communication theory assumes that one person "sends" a message, and the other "receives" the message. In that theory it sounds simple: Sender → message → receiver.

In reality it is not nearly that simple. When the sender sends the message, the receiver does not always receive the message. Rather, the receiver automatically makes an interpretation about what the message means and reacts on the basis of that interpretation. For example, Kenneth asks his wife a "simple" question: "Where did you put the checkbook?" She explodes and says, "Why do you treat me like a child? Why do you assume that I've lost it?" She has made an interpretation about what the question really means. Her interpretation is that it is not really a question, but an accusation. She responds on the basis of her interpretation. Kenneth then counters, "This is why I never talk to you. You always overreact." He has also made an interpretation that she is overly emotional and reactive, and does not even consider the possibility that the way he asked the question, or his tone might have contributed to her interpretation. Now a "simple" question has resulted in a very negative interaction, where both feel completely misunderstood. Two things have blocked understanding and empathy: one is the assumptions and interpretation that were made, and the other is defensiveness. Both made assumptions about what the other was really saying, and then became defensive on the basis of those assumptions.

This simple example illustrates the power of belief systems and of interpretations. Empathic understanding of one's partner is often blocked by automatic interpretations that in turn emerge from belief systems. These belief systems are a significant impediment to the spiritual work of marriage in that they keep us from really understanding our partner. These interpretations usually arise from three types of belief systems: (1) beliefs about marriage, (2) beliefs about our partner, and (3) beliefs about ourselves. Each is capable of leading to the types of automatic interpretations, as in "where's the checkbook" that can block deep knowing or empathic understanding of our partner. These blocks must be worked through so that the spiritual work of really understanding your partner can happen and "I-Thou" moments can occur.

BELIEFS ABOUT MARRIAGE

Ironically, even beliefs about marriage can get in the way of deep understanding of our partner. These beliefs become a filter that then impacts how we see our partner.

For example, if Joe believes that in a good marriage there should not be conflict, then whenever there is conflict he is forced to conclude that he is not in a good marriage. Even worse, if his wife, Brenda, expresses frustration toward him, let alone anger, he is not only left to conclude that he is not in a good marriage, but also that she is not a good wife, and doesn't really love him. At first glance, this seems ridiculous. However, if you think it through more carefully, many of these beliefs about marriage impact the way we see our partners. Several beliefs about marriage can block deep spiritual knowing of our partner just as religious beliefs can often interfere with deep spirituality.

"If you loved me, you would read my mind." In the search for a soul mate, people long for deep empathic attunement for a partner to really know them. However, this belief takes that longing to a new level. In this belief, which most would not admit to, one partner believes that if their partner really loved them, they would be able to read their minds.

Darlene and Bob were driving down the highway, when Darlene exploded. "You knew how much I wanted a cup of coffee, and you drove past the last two rest areas!" Bob, retorted in frustration, "How was I supposed to know that you wanted coffee? You never said a word." Of course, Darlene responded, "After twenty years you should know what I need without me having to tell you."

There are many variations of this belief. However, in the end, they produce the same problematic lack of understanding. Neither Bob nor Darlene was able to really understand each other because of their respective beliefs. Neither was right nor wrong, they were simply guilty of seeing through the lens of their beliefs.

This belief can operate in a wide variety of ways.

Dawn came down with a bad case of the flu and was unable to go work. Her husband George went to work as usual and called around lunchtime to check up on her and they had a brief but pleasant conversation. Unfortunately, at 4:00 p.m., he had a meeting that ran much later than he planned, and didn't get home until around 7:00 p.m. When he finally arrived at home, Dawn was quiet and withdrawn. Internally she was extremely hurt. She was thinking "He knows how sick I am and yet he still puts his business meeting in front of coming home to be with me. If he can't come through for me on something this small, how will I able to trust him with something bigger?" Dawn not only believed that her husband should be able to read her mind and know what she needed, but now had formed another belief: she has lost confidence that her husband can be trusted to meet her deepest needs. This belief could have devastating consequences for their relationship. George, on the other hand, had a similar belief based on his assumptions. He assumed that Dawn would understand how much pressure he was under at work, and how critical this meeting was to his career. Although he was uptight about coming home late, he believed that Dawn should understand that he was under pressure, and so did not talk to her about how torn he felt about his loyalty to her and his pressure at work. He did not even attempt to explain the tension he was feeling as he sat through the meeting, becoming more and more anxious about not being able to leave and get home to his sick wife. He assumed that Dawn understood. However, as he sensed her distance and disappointment, he concluded that he could not trust her enough to share the business pressures he was under or how much anxiety he had been feeling.

Now both Dawn and George had formed new beliefs about each other that would block deep understanding and intimacy, which were at least partially related to their original belief that "if you loved me you would read my mind." Their story illustrates how easy it is for couples to make assumptions and interpretations that in turn leave them distant, and separated from each other. Other couples subscribe to a different belief.

Marriage means we should have everything in common. In this belief, good marriage is defined as two people having everything in common, and of course, on some level there is logic to this. When couples first meet and fall in love they focus on what they have in common and love to do together. Over time, differences emerge. For those who hold this belief system these differences and different interests are viewed as a threat to the marriage, and it is easy to misjudge the other through this belief. Too many people believe that they would be happier if they were married to someone who had more in common with them, and then they begin to believe that the problems they are experiencing in their marriage are related to that. They are not interested then in a deeper understanding of their partner because down deep they really want their partner to be more like them and share their interest. This longing for fusion, or what the psychoanalytic theory of Heinz Kohut (1984) calls the "longing for twinship," blocks deep empathic understanding because differences and different interests are evidence of a relationship that is less than ideal.

Marriage means gender-defined roles. All couples come into marriage with an internal map of what good marriage means, and a model for gender roles within that marriage. These assumptions can easily impact how couples see each other. For example, Lisa assumes that since her husband Jim is not handy or able to fix things like her father, who was able to fix everything around the house and never called a repairman to do anything, he is not a good husband. Similarly, since Lisa is not interested in cooking like his mother, Jim concludes that she is not a good wife.

These beliefs seem simple and obvious. Logically, it would seem simple to negotiate them. However, in reality they are merely a subset of a much bigger problem, and that is the problem of how couples begin to form beliefs about each other. All these simple beliefs about marriage, and many others like them, begin to shift how couples see each other and that is where real distance emerges. As this occurs, it becomes more and more impossible for couples to begin to understand each other in any significant way.

Learning to "see" and truly understand one's partner begins with the recognition that too often these beliefs, and others like them, serve as interpretive filters that block our capacity to truly understand. A first step in moving toward an "I-Thou" relationship involves challenging our beliefs and interpretations that cannot but help turn our partner into an "It" or a category. By beginning to recognize these filters, slowly there is potential to begin to see differently.

THE PROBLEM OF IDEALIZATION
AND INTERPRETATION (LEAVING EDEN)

Most couples begin their relationships with significant idealization. However, it is another and sometimes more insidious block to "seeing" and understanding our partners, which goes all the way back to the beginning of the relationship. This is what is often described as "falling in love." In the falling-in-love stage, couples see each other in an idealized form and are often in a state of fusion. Some liken this to a drug experience. In fact, brain research suggests that a chemical reaction is occurring in the brain that does make it feel like a drug experience. The reality is that it feels so wonderful and idyllic that differences are not visible. The profound, druglike experience of falling in love is all that is seen. Often during premarital therapy, these couples find it difficult to anticipate problems, and enjoy a wonderful sense of fusion and bliss. When asked where they anticipate future problems they are blank; they can only anticipate a wonderful life together. They are in their own Garden of Eden. In the narrative of the Garden of Eden, everything is perfect and innocent, similar to falling in love. Life is wonderful, and couples, like Adam and Eve, anticipate a wonderful future together. However, as in the biblical narrative, the "fall" occurs. It is not surprising that in the narrative, Adam and Even "eat of the Tree of Knowledge," and once they do there is a "fall" that changes everything. They are no longer innocent, no longer fused, and in contrast they begin to blame each other for the problems they are having. Paradise fades and in the story God asks them what happened; Adam is quick to blame Eve and remove himself from responsibility. Similarly, it is so for couples. Over the course of marriage a "fall" occurs. Couples "eat of the Tree of Knowledge," and idealization turns to disillusionment. They begin to see each other in much more realistic ways and begin to see each other's limitations and shortcomings. Little things begin to annoy them, from not picking up things around the house, to the long hours at work, or to the lessoning of conversation. Slowly the "fall" into disillusionment occurs. Traits that were charming have become annoying. Being responsible now looks boring. The humorous spontaneous style that was so endearing in the beginning of the relationship now looks immature. Distance is emerging in the relationship, and assumptions and interpretations are beginning to emerge.

Not only do we lose the idealized picture of our partner that caused us to fall in love, but we are also often deeply wounded that our partner no longer sees us in the way they once did. We sense their irritation and criticism. We long to be seen as good, as lovable, and even as ideal. We wonder if they would choose us again, now that they see us more fully. Like Adam and Eve, not only have we lost the idealized picture we once had of our partner, but also our picture of self—at least as seen through the eyes of our partner is also changed. We long for the days of Eden when we first fell in love.

THE SPIRITUAL OPPORTUNITY

This "fall" is a natural progression for all couples. One of two things is going to happen. For some couples, they will focus more on the differences between them and less on the similarities, and begin to watch their intimacy and connection erode. These couples often hit a tipping point where they begin to lock into negative pictures of each other, which block deep knowing, and have a very negative impact on the relationship. Others, however, will work with the differences and move toward a deeper and more mature form of love. Hopefully, in this journey they will not lose the original spark of falling in love. At that moment of falling in love several things happened. We saw the other as ideal, we felt seen by our partner as ideal, and we saw much in common. This must never be devalued; it is profoundly spiritual. However, it must mature. True spiritual experience does not devalue the original "falling in love," but takes it to a much deeper level. Our picture of our partner (and his or her picture of us) was limited. As we grow, we not only go through some disillusionment, but also can come to see our partner in a much deeper way. True intimacy emerges over time as this happens.

What makes the difference in which way these couples move, since all couples go through some disillusionment in the process of growth? Those couples who move on to a mature form of love have been able to move toward deeper levels of understanding. They have been able to do the profoundly spiritual work of deep empathic understanding. They have found ways to move past their assumptions, and to not lock their partners in rigid frames that limit what they see. They have not been guilty of trying to change their partners into something that they need them to be.

Rather they have learned to listen, and to continue to try to understand on a deep level who their partners are. They have learned to remove the roadblocks to deep understanding.

These couples have found a way to continue to understand their partners on a deeper and deeper level. They will attempt to work through their assumptions and beliefs and practice a deep spirituality to really work at understanding who their partners are. This is hard work indeed and means avoiding many of the typical roadblocks to deep empathic understanding.

THE ROADBLOCKS

Unfortunately, the roadblocks on the journey to deeper levels of empathic understanding are numerous. Consider just a few:

Advice. Some partners are so eager to help that they offer constant advice, which in the end blocks deep empathy.

The Fix-It People. These are individuals who want to fix every problem, without spending time to understand what their partner is really feeling. Like those who offer advice, they often rush toward solutions without stopping to understand. Leroy and Gloria are a good example.

Gloria came home exhausted from teaching her very energetic sixth-grade class. She made a cup of coffee, put her feet up, and described to Leroy how tired she was and how she could not stand one more classroom outburst. "I'm not sure I can keep doing this," she sighed. In response, her husband

Leroy tried to offer some advice in his attempt to fix the problem. "Why don't you set up a new behavior plan?" he suggested. He went on to give his suggestions for what he thought would lower his wife's exhaustion. He of course was in fact trying to be helpful, so he did not understand why his wife exclaimed "Can't you ever just listen? Can't I just complain about my day without you trying to fix it? When I want advice I'll ask for it." Despite Leroy's desire to help his wife, his attempt to help was in the end a great failure of empathy, which of course did not lead to deeper connection.

The roadblocks of advice or trying to fix things are common to many couples. Others attempt to use humor or to avoid conflict at all costs. Still others get so hooked by their own defensiveness that they cannot get past their assumptions and beliefs.

These roadblocks create communication patterns that in the end block meaningful communication and deep understanding. Those who practice the spiritual work of marriage are able to move past these roadblocks, and know and accept their partners deeply.

THE SPIRITUAL OPPORTUNITY

In the end, the spiritual work of marriage is the work of knowing one's partner deeply. It is the work of getting through assumptions and interpretations, and then having a deep empathic understanding of one's partner. This often requires the ability and the courage to deeply work with oneself. In all of the case examples, the well-meaning partners are struggling with an anxiety that is threatening to their sense of self (i.e., If my partner is unhappy, or if I realize that I am helpless in the face of her pain, I will die. I will not be able to handle it, she won't love me anymore, etc.). The spiritual journey requires courage and self-focus and the ability to face these fears and anxieties. Several steps are necessary to begin the process.

1. Recognize that the longing to be known is among the most powerful of all human desires.
2. Begin to take steps to help your partner be known by working at trying to fully enter his or her subjective world. Work on listening, asking questions, and checking in with questions like "Do you feel like I'm getting it?"
3. Begin to recognize the filters that you are seeing your partner through and work at shifting them.

4. Begin to recognize the roadblocks that you use that may be impacting your ability to listen.
5. Ask your partner for feedback about what he or she needs.
6. Finally, recognize that this is in the end profoundly spiritual work. It is connecting to the deepest spiritual and relational need. It is being incarnational. It is connecting to the longing of the Psalmist who says of being known, "Such knowledge is too wonderful for me, too lofty for me to attain" (Psalm 139:6 [NIV]).

The chapters that follow explore other spiritual tasks and challenges that must be accomplished to move toward this deep understanding and acceptance and profoundly spiritual work.

Chapter 3

The Idolatry of Attempting to Change Your Partner

The "Gospel" according to family systems theory: the only person you can ever change is you.

Idolatry: ". . . the visual or mental representation. It may refer to the object that is seen or the mental representation of it that the observer forms in his mind."

Brown, 1971

Listen to couples during the falling-in-love stage. Their descriptions of each other are idyllic. They cannot spend enough time together hanging out, talking, exploring interests, and planning a life together. Most couples are not thinking during the wedding ceremony, "I hope that he is going to learn to listen sometime," or "I hope he learns to be responsible," or "I hope she stops calling her mother." If they are thinking these thoughts as the organ plays "Here comes the bride," they are certainly in trouble; usually at that moment most couples are thinking about how perfect their partner is.

Being known and understood and accepted is a universal longing. Knowing that your partner wants you to change is the antithesis of being known and accepted. Not to mention, anyone who has been married for a long time can attest to the futility of trying to change their partner. Talk to any older couple who has been married for a long time, and ask them how much success they have had in molding their partners. Most would just laugh. Many begin the journey of marriage assuming that over time they will succeed in changing their partner, along with his or her annoying habits; those who have been married for any length of time know how impossible that is. In fact, the opposite is true. Paradoxically, the harder you try to change someone the more he or she stays the same. Despite this reality, most will continue their futile quest while becoming more and more frustrated in the process. In reality, this attempt to change one's partner will always limit and block deep understanding and empathy. Therefore, for couples who want to move toward the spiritual practice of deep understanding and empathy for their partners, working through the desire to change one's partner is critical.

THE FIRST RULE OF RELATIONSHIPS

Intellectually, it is easy to accept the first fundamental rule of relationships: *The only person you can change is you.* However, understanding this rule as an intellectual theory and living it out in reality are two different things. Much of the pain of relationship comes from misguided attempts to change your partner.

Julia was a bright, vivacious educator, but she was increasingly frustrated with her husband John. Julia was outgoing, charming, funny, and could talk to anyone. John was an introvert, who loved to read, and escape into his thoughts. The thought of going to a party was torture for him. His idea of a great weekend was doing some yard work, reading, and working in his shop in the basement. Julia, on the other hand, loved to go out with friends and do social things on the weekend. Obviously they were stuck. Julia, down deep, was convinced that she could change John. She complained that he wasn't trying to be social and that he was just too cognitive. She pushed, pleaded, and cajoled, which just made John more quiet and resentful. Julia could not recognize that she was actually making the problem worse with her misguided attempts to change her husband. She was certainly not working hard to enter his world and better understand him; she was much more interested in changing him.

Try to picture your own attempts to change your partner. How successful were you? Trying to get your partner to share his or her feelings more deeply, or be less emotional, or spend more time with you, or give you more space, or be neater around the house, or practice greater levels of financial responsibility, etc., almost never work. You begin to believe that the key to marital happiness is persuading your partner to change to your specs. Unfortunately, this almost always makes things worse. The harder you try to create change the more negative your partner appears, and the more both of you feel deeply misunderstood.

At times, this dubious enterprise looks hopeful. Occasionally, it appears that your partner is actually changing. Usually, after a fight or crisis, there is a commitment made by both partners to seriously change. Yet this change usually is short-lived. Those promises to spend more time talking, or keep the house neater, or not use the credit card, or pledges to make a greater attempt to not talk negatively about the in-laws all sound good. However, they usually do not last. Family systems theory calls this *homeostasis:* the more things change the more they eventually drift back to the way they were in the beginning. Just like a thermostat keeps the heat at a relatively constant temperature, relationships have their own built-in thermostats, which keep things more or less the same. There are many examples of this. Consider just a few:

Alice pleads with her husband to get home from work at a decent hour and spend time with her and the kids. After several late-night emotional arguments, her husband Dan eventually agrees to try harder. For a few weeks he is home at a decent hour, but as their relationship calms down, the old pattern slowly reemerges.

* * *

Paul finally convinces his wife Ellen to work-out with him at the local gym, but then is discouraged when she slowly loses interest. On the other hand, Ellen has tried for years to drag Paul to the opera. When he finally agrees to go, he falls asleep in the first hour.

* * *

Johan is constantly frustrated that his wife does not want to spend more time talking with him. He feels more and more wounded by what he considers to be her emotional distancing from him. He pleads, and without meaning to, nags her to spend more time talking to him. Li Ming feels pressured by his nagging and ironically shuts down more. She believes that no matter how she tries her attempts will not be enough. Thus, though there are small moments of change, for the most part, things come back to the same place in the relationship.

There are countless examples of couples' well-intentioned efforts to change their partner. Fill in the following blank in terms of how you try to change your partner: "If you would just _____." Down deep you believe that if your partner would just change your marriage would improve.

If our partners would just change, we would be happier and have a more fulfilling relationship. Thus our happiness is contingent on the efforts of our partner, which is always dangerous. Yet the more pressure we create the worse things get. Paradoxically, the harder we try the more we guarantee that things will stay the same. Hence, the obvious first rule of relationships: *The only person you can change is you.*

THE ELUSIVE SEARCH FOR PERFECTION: A SPIRITUAL AND RELATIONAL PROBLEM

Couples frequently misunderstand the significant spiritual challenges that are part of marital problems. *What most people crave in the depths of their being is the experience of being accepted simply for who they are, and not for who their partner hopes they will be.* People want not only to be understood, but also accepted. The theological word for this is "grace." Grace means being accepted at the core of your being, not because of anything you have done or are becoming. It means being understood and being accepted as you are. As a result, this spiritual task of marriage can be extremely difficult. This task involves offering acceptance rather than attempting to change the other into what we think we need. Just the thought of that can create anxiety.

The biblical concept for attempting to change one's partner is idolatry. Kathleen Norris (1998) describes it in *Amazing Grace: A Vocabulary of Faith.*

> The idea of that person—and "idea" is related etymologically to the word "idol"—becomes more important, more potent than the actual living creature. It is much safer to love an idol than a real live person who is capable of surprising you, loving you and demanding love in return, and maybe one day leaving you. (p. 90)

Most people would have a difficult time applying this concept to marriage and specifically to attempts to change their partner. Most do not take the time to consider that attempting to change their partner is in fact not only impossible, but also a spiritual problem. In order to further understand this, it is important to examine what the word *idolatry* actually means from an Old Testament perspective.

BIBLICAL IDOLATRY

The words "image" and "idol" are often used interchangeably in the Old Testament. According to the *New International Dictionary of New Testament Theology* (Brown, 1971), the words "suggest a visual or mental representation. It may refer to the object that is seen or the mental representation of it that the observer forms in his mind" (vol. 2, p. 284). An image or idol is a representation of the real person, but in fact is not the real person. In marriage, we begin to push our partner to be the representation that we think we need; unfortunately some of this is not even conscious. For many reasons, which will be discussed later in this book, we believe that our partner should match our mental representation of what an ideal partner should be. In short, we create our own idol and then push our partner to be that, which of course never works.

Like the ancient Israelites in the story that follows, when anxious, we believe that we will be happier if our partner becomes more of what we need him or her to be. Unfortunately, there is a great cost to this enterprise. As with all idols, the reality of who our partner really is gets lost. As described in the last chapter, when the essence of the other is lost, he or she becomes an "It" in the words of Martin Buber (1996), not a "Thou." Experiencing one's partner as a "Thou" is to listen, accept, and discover the depths of the person we love. When we try to change, and nag and mold the person we turn our partner into an "It."

The Story of the Golden Calf

Think about how this idea worked in the Old Testament story of Moses and the creation of the golden calf (Exodus 32:1-8). According to the story, Moses had been on Mt. Sinai for a long time speaking with God and receiving the Ten Commandments. In his absence, the Israelites became extremely anxious and frightened. Their leader was gone, and they saw no evidence of the presence of God. In the psychoanalytic theory of object relations, they did not have "object constancy." Object constancy, for example, is the experience of the toddler who grows up in a healthy family with a healthy mother. The infant feels secure even when its mother is gone for a period of time because the image of its mother has been sufficiently internalized resulting in object constancy and security. This child does not experience acute separation anxiety each time he or she is separated from its mother, because he or she knows that mom will return. The Israelites did not have object constancy in their relationship to God and so when their leader Moses was gone, they suffered separation anxiety. In their anxiety, they believed they must do something. They needed an image or representation of a God that was more visible, more tangible, in short—more what they believed they needed God to be. Therefore, they melted down their jewelry and created a golden calf. They temporarily contained their anxiety by creating a golden calf (the God they thought they needed), but the bad news is they lost the essence of God. They created an "It" and lost the "Thou" (to borrow again from Martin Buber, 1996). Obviously, the story has a bad ending and a lot of warnings about the danger of idolatry. The Israelites replaced God with a "golden calf" modeled after their need for an idolatrous image. God as "Thou" was reduced to God as "It" with dangerous consequences.

Due to significant anxiety, the ancient Israelites could not accept the God they knew and who had led them out of Egypt; as a result, they attempted to shape and mold a God that was more congruent with what they thought they needed. In the end, the God they created (the golden calf) was of course incapable of giving them what they needed. This is so with marriage when we pressure our partners to be what we think we need them to be; we destroy their ability to give us what we really crave—intimacy. Partners who feel pressured to change are incapable of intimacy.

Both the first rule of relationship "the only person you can change is you" and the corresponding spiritual task of working toward acceptance versus trying to change our partner into the idol that we think they need to be are necessary lessons of moving toward intimacy.

Intimacy and Idolatry

In the end it is impossible to find intimacy with an idol, or with a person you have molded, even if you are successful in changing your partner. Intimacy is the by-product of deep sharing and deep acceptance. Our attempts to change our partner are both a serious spiritual problem and a move away from the intimacy that we crave. David Schnarch (1997), in his book *Passionate Marriage,* argues that intimacy is only possible with people who are capable of fully holding onto themselves and who can nonreactively be themselves in relationship. Attempting to change one's partner is a move away from intimacy.

Consider what happens when you continue to try to change your partner. Not only do you paradoxically make change impossible, certain relationship patterns form that eventually define the relationship thus making it more and more difficult to both receive acceptance or to offer it to our partners. Ironically, that which we want most is blocked by our misguided attempts to change our partners.

HOPELESS DANCES

Think of what happens in our relationships when we feel insecure or anxious. Like the story of the golden calf, we try to create an idol by changing our partner. Yet in the process, relationship patterns take on a life of their own. Consider several powerful relationship patterns.

The Pursuer-Distancer Dance

Perhaps the most obvious example of a relationship pattern that takes on a life of its own is the pursuer-distancer pattern. This pattern has received much attention in the marriage and family therapy literature. It is an excellent example of what happens when the proposed solution to the problem actually becomes the problem. It is one natural outgrowth of a well-meaning attempt to change your partner in the interest of creating intimacy.

Beth craved a more intimate relationship with her husband Robert. Although she remembers that early in their relationship it seemed that they could talk for hours and that Robert was her best friend, now, fifteen years later, she described him as distant, remote, and emotionally unavailable. Her intention of trying recapture the closeness of their early years was well-meaning and certainly well-intentioned. Early on, when she first noticed that their marriage was becoming more distant and formal, she attempted to persuade Robert to spend more time talking with her, and tried to prepare romantic dinners for the two of them as a way of setting the stage for more relaxed conversation. Frequently these dinners left her disappointed as Robert seemed tired and suggested putting the news on before dinner was over. Over time, her attempts to change Robert and create more intimacy turned more critical, and she began criticizing Robert for being distant and disinterested. His response would often be equally critical, "If you would just get off my back I'd want to talk more to you." "The only time you want to talk to me is when you want sex" would be Beth's angry response. The result was obvious—both would retreat and become more distant. Their solution had now become the problem. The more Beth pursued and tried to get Robert to spend more time talking the more he distanced and asked for more space. Of course the more he distanced the more she in turn pursued. Their mutual attempt to change each other simply created distance, and made intimacy impossible.

The pursuer-distancer dance is a classic example of one relationship pattern that emerges in the attempt to create relationship change by trying to change one's partner. Attempts at change simply result in a pattern that becomes bigger than both partners. Unfortunately, in relationships, one plus one does not equal two. Rather, two people attempting to create an intimate relationship end up cocreating a relationship pattern that is bigger than both parties. This dance takes on a life of its own, and further blocks intimacy and change. The pursuer-distancer dance is a classic example of this pattern. In the end, the harder one attempts to pursue in the interest of change the more the other distances.

Other similar patterns are easily created. Consider several other patterns that easily emerge and define relationships. These patterns are described in great detail in my earlier book, *The Couple's Survival Workbook,* and will be described only briefly here (Olsen and Stephens, 2001).

The Over-Under Responsible Pattern

In the over-under responsible pattern one partner takes on a disproportionate amount of the responsibility, all the while being critical of his or her partner for not creating more balance. The other partner appears then to be the underresponsible one and feels constantly criticized. At the same time, when the underresponsible partner attempts to create more relationship balance and volunteers to take on more of the responsibility around the house, the overresponsible partner has a difficult time letting go. As a result both are frustrated and angry. They both complain about their partner. The underresponsible person complains that his or her partner is no fun, is always uptight, and can never relax and enjoy life. Of course, the overresponsible partner insists that he or she can't relax because he or she has to be responsible for everything.

In the end, neither "see" their partner. Both are frustrated and wish their partner were different. Spiritually, they are unable to either deeply understand their partner let alone offer any acceptance to the other. Their dance has defined them and there is no grace or acceptance in the relationship.

Systems theory reminds us that in marriage one plus one does not equal two. The reality of marriage is that the sum is greater than the parts. Two people, in their efforts to change each other end up cocreating a relationship pattern, which in the end blocks them from really seeing each other, let alone offering acceptance. These patterns become a type of dance that in the end takes on a life of its own. To illustrate this reality, think about your most predictable marital argument. If you are honest, you can probably predict how it will start, what you will say and how your partner will respond, how it will escalate, and how it will end. Rarely does new information emerge, and seldom does creative resolution occur. The reality is your "dance" has developed a life of its own.

The Dance Blocks Acceptance

Unfortunately, in the futile effort to change each other, couples inevitably recreate the status quo by cocreating patterns or "the dance." There are a number of types of dances. They include the two that have just been described as well as several others such as the dominant-submissive pattern where one partner is seen as dominant and the other gives in. Or, the fight-or-flight pattern where one wants to fight, or at least wants to assertively tackle the problems, while the other avoids conflict (these patterns are described in great detail in *The Couple's*

Survival Workbook, by Olsen and Stephens, 2001). All of these patterns reinforce each other, create homeostasis, and block acceptance from being offered.

Even when couples use the same style, they end up creating homeostasis. For example, the rapid-escalator couple reinforce each other by together rapidly escalating every argument into a major problem. Together they pour fuel on the fire of even the smallest conflict until eventually it is blazing out of control.

On the other extreme is the conflict-avoidant couple. This couple maintains a polite homeostasis by avoiding any significant potential conflict. In so doing they are able to maintain polite homeostasis at the cost of intimacy.

The Dance Prevents Acceptance and Grace

When people attempt to change each other they create patterned dances or relationship patterns, precluding the acceptance they crave. In reality, these patterns trap couples into reinforcing the very things they are trying to change. For example, the more the pursuer pursues the more he or she teaches his or her partner to distance. The more the partner distances, the more he or she is inadvertently training his or her partner to pursue. One reinforces the other.

Too often, solutions to the problems of life actually become the problems themselves. The harder you try to change your partner the more the very process of trying becomes the problem and further blocks change. In the end, the spiritual and relational tragedy is that neither partner feels accepted nor is the recipient of grace.

The spiritual work of marriage begins with recognizing the futility of trying to change one's partner. It begins by recognizing the "dance" or relational pattern that emerges from the attempt. Recognize that the only person you can change is you; begin by changing your role in the dance. If, for example, you are a pursuer, try holding back. If you are overresponsible, experiment with delegating. If you tend to distance and withdraw, try occasionally changing the dance and initiating more contact.

The spiritual work of marriage involves moving away from these destructive attempts to change one's partner and toward offering acceptance and grace.

Consider taking the following action steps:

- Recognize that accepting your partner as he or she is a spiritual opportunity and certainly represents spiritual work. Therefore, trying to change your partner is a form of idolatry and is always a spiritual and relational block.
- Recognize your "idolatrous" attempts to change your partner and understand how it is part of your own anxiety. It is only when you begin to focus on yourself and your own anxiety that you can understand why you need to try to change your partner.
- Have the courage to focus only on yourself, and attempt to shift your part of these dangerous relationship patterns by focusing only on yourself and your own contributions.
- Practice focusing on the positive qualities of your partner and attempt to offer acceptance wherever you can. In reality, how we see things can determine our reality. If all we focus on is what we really want to change with our partner, then we see only the negative. On the other hand, when we remember what drew us to our partner originally, then we can begin to see more creatively.

Chapter 4

The Sins of the Fathers
and the Longing for Redemption

Redemption: To loose, untie, set free, release, buy back, annul.

Brown, 1971, p. 177

For I the Lord your God am a jealous God, visiting the iniquity of the fathers upon the sons to the third and fourth generation. . . .

Exodus 20:5 (NIV)

The sins of the father are to be laid upon the children.

Shakespeare, *The Merchant of Venice,* Act III, Sc. V, l. 1

Multigenerational Transmission—the pattern that develops over multiple generations as children emerge from the parental family with higher, equal, or lower basic levels of differentiation than the parents.

Bowen and Kerr, 1988, p. 477

Sondra and Alex had a goal: they wanted to change history. They both had grown up in alcoholic, abusive families. They were intelligent and determined professionals who were determined to create a far better life than they had grown up with. Sondra summed up their feelings speaking with soft defiance, "It stops with us. Our kids are not going to experience what we experienced. They will have a different childhood and a different future." They wanted redemption from the wounds of the generations that preceded them.

It was a great plan with great passion behind it. The problem was—it wasn't working. Like many couples they longed to be understood by each other and create a wonderful atmosphere for their kids, but were very discouraged. Despite wonderful goals and great energy, they felt defeated. Their marriage was on the verge of coming apart. Sondra summed it up, "We tried so hard, but I can't keep doing this. We are just not connected. Alex seems to be angry all the time, and ignores me. I don't know what else to do."

What had gone wrong? This couple had done everything right. They went through premarital counseling, took a course in communication skills, and had even read several marital self-help books as well as books on alcoholic families. Despite these efforts they were coming apart. Their depression was palpable. After several minutes of silence Alex expressed what both of them were feeling. "We know what divorce does to kids. It was horrible watching our parents separate. Now look at us, have we become as our parents? We don't want the same thing to happen to our children." How do couples like Alex and Sondra fail to change history despite their best efforts? Why, despite all their hard work and commitment, was their marriage not working?

What Alex and Sondra are longing for is to break the cycle of dysfunctional family patterns. They are longing to escape the words of the Old Testament writer who predicted that the "sins of the fathers" would be visited on future generations. Alex and Sondra wanted to escape the curse of the "sins" of their parents; they wanted redemption.

THE POWER OF FAMILY OF ORIGIN

Family is powerful. That of course is an understatement. Just think of what happens when you return home to the family you grew up with for any extended period of time. Within three days, it is easy to feel like you are fifteen again. Suddenly, and without warning, you are feeling just as reactive and agitated as you did when you were growing up. What makes it so intense?

Our families shape us in so many ways. It is one thing to describe the struggle for acceptance and deep empathic understanding, as well as to describe the struggles to attempt to change each other, it is another to understand the origins of those struggles.

For most people, these struggles emerged from their experience of growing up. Problems that were unresolved in family of origin can become marital issues. Too often couples hope to get from their partners what they didn't get from their parents. Sondra summed it up:

"My father was constantly critical and angry. I could never do anything right no matter how hard I tried. I brought home great report cards, never got in trouble, and tried to take care of my brothers. However, he never noticed and then just left when I was fifteen." She began to cry softly and tried to compose herself. "Even though he was such a jerk, I wanted him to notice what I was doing." She hesitated and then added, "But now I feel the same way with Alex. I feel almost invisible to him—he doesn't notice or appreciate anything I do, and can always find the one thing I haven't done to be critical of." In an uncanny replication, Alex was repeating what her father had done.

Despite their work and efforts to communicate, Sondra felt hurt by her husband in the same ways that she had been hurt as a child. This is the mystery and heartbreak of marriage. Despite the best of efforts of both, they were unsuccessful in breaking this cycle.

THE SPIRITUAL WORK OF REDEMPTION

What couples long for from their partners is healing, healing that helps to rework old pain and hurt from earlier in life or childhood. This is the spiritual work of redemption. Couples, like Alex and Sondra, hope that their partners will not hurt them the way their parents did and that they will be instruments of healing and redemption. They are longing for their partners to help them heal, which in the end is spiritual work. Unfortunately, like Sondra and Alex, this is often not understood and is usually unconscious, but it is powerful nonetheless. It is too easy for couples like Sondra and Alex to feel deep sadness when they realize they have recreated old, painful patterns. At times they may even feel hopeless about themselves, their partner, or their future. Until they understand the complexity of family-of-origin issues, it can often feel overwhelming. In order to fully understand this longing for redemption and not give in to hopelessness, it is necessary to understand the complexities of the internalized family map.

THE FAMILY MAP

Unfortunately, no matter how far people move away from their family of origin, they take their family with them. Even when parents are deceased their powerful influence lives on because parents and family history live on within everyone. The experiences of growing up form a type of internal relationship map that has great impact on marriage. This map contains roles, rules, and often, old injuries, which in turn lead to defense mechanisms, which are attempts to cope with the hurt.

How many times have you heard someone say (or said it yourself) "My marriage will be totally different from that of my parents," or "I will never marry someone like my father." Yet despite sincere efforts to create something different, too often, the past is recreated. This is the legacy of the family map. That map, unconscious as it might be, has great power and is comprised of many powerful beliefs that were formed by family of origin and are now deeply internalized. Of course, these beliefs have great influence within marriage. There are many examples of these beliefs such as "discussing money leads to fighting," "keep negative feelings to yourself," "getting all your feelings out during a fight clears the air and everyone feels better," "trusting people will always get you hurt," "men should make the financial decisions." The list could go on and on.

Unfortunately, these beliefs become a filter through which we see our partners. We explored in a previous chapter how these beliefs and interpretations block us from seeing and deeply understanding our partner. If for example, you believe that talking about money leads to powerful conflict then you will not talk about money.

This map is powerfully formed in childhood as we watch and listen to family members. Growing up, we listen and observe the way family members talk to one another: the way they touch (or don't), the way conflict is handled, and how intimacy is expressed. These messages are both direct and indirect. If, for example, a child hears his parents argue, then observes silence for several days and then things go back to normal, he assumes that that is the norm for how conflict is handled. If parents never touch or are not demonstrative, then another lesson is filed away. All these mini lessons are internalized and form a comprehensive family map.

The great family therapist Murray Bowen (Bowen and Kerr, 1988) taught that our identities and core beliefs emerge from our experience with our family, and that these experiences have been shaped by the generations that in turn preceded them. This family environment not only forms a relationship map that guides many of our actions and decisions in marriage, but that map is also shaped by many previous generations. No wonder it is so powerful. Despite their great intentions this is what Sondra and Alex did not understand. In their naiveté they hoped that simply attempting to build something different than their parents would be sufficient. They were not aware of the internalized relationship map that was guiding them far more than they realized.

FAMILY RITUALS

A "simple" example explores the way this map works.

Despite a childhood that was less the optimal, birthdays in Sondra's house were a huge deal. Despite alcoholism and other significant problems, the family managed to pull together on birthdays, and they would be an enormous event. In contrast, in Alex's family, birthdays were low-key, with no big celebration and maybe one or two small presents. As a result, in the first few years of their marriage, Sondra would be deeply hurt that Alex did not create a large birthday celebration for her, and then Alex would simmer in resentment not knowing why she had to make such a big deal over her birthday. He eventually blurted out, "Why don't you grow up? At thirty-one shouldn't you have outgrown this?" Of course this just added to Sondra's pain.

It wasn't just that Sondra wanted a large birthday party. It was more that she wanted Alex to understand her and know what she needed. She wished he could understand that birthdays were the one positive memory that she had as a child. She wanted Alex to make her feel visible and special. When he did not make her birthday more special, she felt like he didn't understand her and, worse, that he just didn't care. When he got angry at her for being hurt, she felt hopeless and began to withdraw physically and emotionally. It would be easy to reduce this problem into a simple issue of how to work out a birthday celebration, but that would miss the more important point. Their problem is much more about childhood maps and the longing for redemption. It was about Sondra longing to be deeply understood, about holding onto one positive part of her childhood, and about wanting to know that she was not only special but also really understood by her husband. The birthday issues were simply a manifestation of all of that. Without being able to verbalize it, she longed for Alex to understand her and all of the pain with which she had grown up and to somehow help to redeem it. Yet their mutual family maps had left them trapped in a cycle of misunderstanding and blame. It wasn't that Alex didn't want to understand. He certainly wanted to be loving and understanding of his wife. However, the power of their mutual internalized family maps was taking over.

ROLES AND SCRIPTS

This map can also govern family roles. Growing up, kids are "assigned" roles. How this happens is a mystery, but for most it does happen. One child becomes the "good child" who then becomes the peacemaker, trying to avoid all conflict and keep the family functioning smoothly. "Good" children are afraid to fully express themselves or their feelings because they need to keep everything peaceful. Another child is "assigned" the mantle of success and feels obligated to be successful on behalf of the family. This child feels both anxiety and pressure to be successful and tends to overfunction in many parts of his or her life. Another takes on the role of the rebel, and tends to get in trouble and seems to constantly challenge authority.

The problem, of course, is that these roles follow us throughout life. The good child tends to remain conflict avoidant and remains concerned about doing everything right and keeping things calm. They often continue to take on the burden of being peacemakers and avoiding conflict. The overfunctioner certainly does not stop overfunctioning as an adult. They tend to continue to overfunction in their many roles in adult life, sometimes despite great exhaustion. These roles not only follow people throughout life, but can also, all too easily, become traps that are difficult to escape. How often does the overfunctioner complain about how exhausted he or she is, and yet continue to overfunction and take on yet another task?

One of the longings for redemption is to be set free from the old roles that have too easily become a trap. Part of longing is for our partner to understand and help free us from the role we are trapped in. For example, between the 1930s and 1980s, many people collected Green Stamps. Green Stamps were a form of trading stamp. When you had a certain number of stamps you could take them to a "redemption center" where you could "purchase" certain awards or products. In marriage, the longing for redemption brings these old wounds and old roles to marriage with the hope of trading them for something better. Andrea was a good example.

Andrea was constantly smiling and always charming; few people ever realized how exhausted she was behind her smile. People constantly complimented her on how positive she was and wondered how she was able to do it all. She kept her house impeccable, her three kids always seemed to be doing well, and her job as a principal of a difficult school kept her working long hours. On the surface she seemed to do it all—despite how impossible that seemed. What she had a difficult time admitting was that in reality she was tired most of the time. Not simply physically tired, but mentally exhausted. Having grown up as the eldest child in a poor family with a mentally ill mother, she had always kept the family together. She parented everyone, including her mother from her earliest memories. She was her father's confidant when he felt like he couldn't cope any more. All of her relatives admired her and described her as the child that would "go places." She did—but at a great cost. Her own needs rarely got met, and she worked so hard that she rarely knew what those needs were most of the time. Secretly she hoped her husband Mike would understand and try to help create balance. Unlike Andrea, he certainly knew how to relax. He worked a low-stress job, played in a golf league, and assumed that his wife was more than capable of doing most of the parenting and the housework. His friends loved hanging out with him because he was always relaxed and low key. Andrea resented the imbalance in their lives, but when she would try to talk about it Mike would tell her that she should learn to relax and take up a hobby. He always had a list of ways that she could take up a new hobby to help her relax, but never realized that she could not even imagine fitting in one more thing, even if it was for fun. What she wanted was redemption. She wanted Mike to understand how trapped she was in her overfunctioning role and desperately needed help finding balance. In some ways she wanted to be more like him, but he became one more person that she was taking care of. She did not need suggestions on yet another thing to take on, but a partner to help take on more of the responsibilities; a partner who would understand her level of exhaustion. Redemption for Andrea would be to be released from a powerful childhood role with significant help from her partner; the reality is that redemption needed to come from outside of her. Her husband needed to understand how hard it had been for her and how trapped in her role she had been and then take steps to help create a change.

Initially, part of Andrea's attraction to Mike was that she saw him as a person who would help her heal. Yet it became one more relationship where she ended up repeating old roles one more time and feeling even more hurt that even her husband did not understand.

Like Andrea, many hope that in marriage they will be redeemed or set free from old roles. Unfortunately, they, like Andrea, are often disappointed and hurt. For this to happen, their partner must be able to see and understand what they need, and they need to be able to better communicate what they need. Yet so often the old roles are so powerful that people are blind to both what they need as well as how best to communicate this to their partner. The patterns that we become trapped in keep us trapped in the same painful roles.

REDEMPTION FROM CHILDHOOD WOUNDS

This longing for redemption also speaks to old childhood injuries. Andrea is also a good example of that. Because she was so successful, and functioned at such a high level, very few people understood the level of pain she experienced. In fact, much of the time, Andrea blocked this from herself. She was so busy all of the time that she rarely slowed down long enough to feel much of anything.

However, Andrea is a powerful example of how roles that are taken in childhood also function as a defense against significant pain and injury. The reality of course, for Andrea, is that childhood had been incredibly painful, but her adult life was so busy that she did not have time to really be in touch with that pain. However, when she began to describe it, she began to cry. She described the terror she felt living with a mentally ill mother, who frequently went off her medication. During those times, Andrea would try to protect her siblings and comfort them. She described her chronic anxiety coming home from school every day, not knowing what she would find. She described times when her mother would come into her room in the middle of the night and tell Andrea that she might commit suicide. At other times she would go into irrational rages at almost nothing. Andrea described how terrorized she felt because she had no idea of what to do. At the same time she felt obligated to calm her siblings so that they would be able to get to sleep. Her father was also part of the problem because he would regularly confide in Andrea that he didn't know what to do with her mother and how overwhelmed he was. He would compliment her by saying, "I don't know what I would do without you. You seem to always know what to do with her." This "compliment" unfortunately did two things: it reinforced Andrea's overfunctioning role and made her special. In addition, it blocked her from being a child and from her fears and insecurities being responded to. Andrea was there for her parents; they were not there for her. This reversal of the parenting function will always leave deep injuries. As a result, Andrea was left both with significant wounds and a powerful defensive role—being the overfunctioning member of the family. Did that defensive role work? Absolutely, but that was the problem. It worked too well. She became so good at her role, and the way it blocked her deep wounds, that it now had become the problem. She was trapped by her childhood role, exhausted, increasingly anxious, and very lonely. It was all catching up. Without even knowing what she was looking for, she longed for redemption on two levels. First, she needed help being released from her powerful childhood role as overfunctioner. Second, she needed her husband to understand how tired and vulnerable she really was and not repeat the same mistakes as her father, by reinforcing her in this powerful role. She needed Mike to know that she really wasn't Wonder Woman. This could be a powerful opportunity for healing and redemption for this couple, but it was contingent on Mike understanding or Andrea being clear enough in her communication to help him get it.

Andrea's story is not unique; like Andrea, everyone comes into marriage with some injury or pain, and a clear role. For some it is more obvious and more severe than others. For many, they come into marriage hoping for some redemption for both. Unfortunately, this remains out of conscious awareness. Andrea felt more and more hurt and angry at Mike's inability to understand what she needed. However, at the same time, she did not know how to even begin to describe the trap she was in. She had no experience to draw on of even beginning to describe what she needed, since for most of her life she overfunctioned on behalf of everyone else.

THE GOAL OF REDEMPTION IN MARRIAGE

Like Andrea, most people long to be redeemed or released from old roles, from old rules, and healed from old injuries. Unfortunately, these desires are rarely verbalized and sometimes not understood. Too many intense couple conflicts focus on surface problems because the couple is unable to fully understand and communicate about deeper issues. Although Andrea would never dream of talking to Mike about all that she needed, on some level she hoped that he would understand. However, Mike was too busy enjoying his life, and his wife seemed to have everything working so well.

The work of redemption begins with couples, like Mike and Andrea, thinking and talking about what they really want and need from each other. It involves slowing down, becoming more *non*reactive, and beginning to honestly explore what they need from each other. Books such as *Getting the Love That You Want* (Hendrix, 1988) can be useful to couples in helping them better understand and communicate what they want and need.

However, this is where the work gets extremely difficult. We are all initially attracted to someone whom we think will "redeem" us from old roles and from old wounds. We hope, often unconsciously, that we will find healing and redemption. Too often, instead of finding redemption, we find ourselves locked into old roles even more and too frequently find ourselves being re-wounded. Andrea, for example, never dreamed that she would find herself trapped in the same exhausting role that she was trapped in as a child, nor did she ever think she would find herself re-wounded. Never in her fantasies about marriage did she envision herself trapped in the same exhausting, over-functioning role that she had grown up in.

Although the earlier steps of empathic attunement (really getting to know your partner) and letting go of futile attempts to change your partner are important first steps, redemption speaks to the possibility of transformation and profound spiritual work. As partners become more conscious of the pain they brought into their marriage and their idealized wish for their partner to be what they never had, they can begin to see their partner as a helper on their spiritual path. This is a very humbling experience, because it means not only letting go of the dream of the ideal partner you longed for, but also letting go of some pictures of self that are not accurate. It means accepting responsibility for our own brokenness, flaws, and humanness. We are not ideal either and at times that can be very difficult to accept. Redemption begins by turning inward and is a significant part of the journey.

To do the spiritual work of redemption, couples need to understand both themselves and their partner, and to understand the longing for healing and for redemption. It is too easy to get caught up in the realities of everyday life, and find a comfortable (or uncomfortable) homeostasis, and lose touch with the deeper longings in ourselves and in our partners. The result of this homeostasis is a lost opportunity for profound spiritual work that will lead to deeper levels of intimacy. Initially, this was the case with Andrea and Mike. They became trapped in the realities of everyday life, and lived on the surface without deep understanding and communication about what was missing.

Spiritual work is always about a journey inward to better understand the depths within us as well as a journey toward others. Without that journey, spiritual work, like redemption, cannot occur.

ACTION STEPS

Two steps are necessary for redemption to take place, and they are both difficult. Step one is personal responsibility, or what the late family therapist Murray Bowen called "differentiation." Step two focuses on the need for empathic attunement, i.e., really knowing what your partner needs and helping them ask for it (Bowen and Kerr, 1988).

Differentiation is, according to Bowen family therapists, a lifelong journey. It is the capacity to fully hold onto yourself and to what you need, while remaining emotionally connected to your partner. The definition sounds easy; however, it is not easy to enact. Too often we feel pressured by what our partner needs or become trapped in the type of mutually reinforcing counterproductive cycles that we described in the previous chapter. The more we are trapped in those reactive cycles the less clear we become about what we need and what we want. The greater the degree of reactivity the less clear we become. This was certainly true for Andrea. She did not want to cause conflict with her husband, and knew that if she were more assertive about what she needed in terms of balance it would disrupt the balance and rhythm of their lives together and potentially cause conflict and tension. Although she was exhausted, she did not want to disrupt their lives. Differentiation for Andrea would mean being able to take a risk, deal with some anxiety, and nonreactively hold on to what she needed from Mike. She would have to take a clear position and ask for concrete change. For example, she could ask Mike to take on more of the specific household responsibilities. However, once she did she would have to stay nonreactive if he became defensive. Even more difficult would be to nonreactively hold onto what she needed until some compromise was reached. This is extremely difficult work. In the end, what Andrea wanted was not just to have a better sense of role sharing, but to feel understood and redeemed by her husband in terms of her old roles and rules.

Step two is for Mike to be able to do that. He too must learn to be differentiated. When Andrea first approached him about sharing more in the household tasks, he became immediately defensive. "Why are you bringing this up now? I've been trying to do more around the house, and I'm more busy at work than I've ever been before." This response could easily launch the couple into a patterned argument that would certainly go nowhere. The task for Mike is to actually understand that he is not being criticized. He will need to understand that in the end this is not simply about better balance but about Andrea being understood. If he does not become defensive and really attempts to listen, he might begin to understand the exhaustion caused by that hypervigilance with which his wife has been living with all her life.

If he can really get it and practice the deep empathic attunement discussed in previous chapters, he can help his wife find redemption and healing. Redemption, in this case, would mean that Andrea would feel deeply understood and would slowly begin to find better balance in her life and even find rest.

Chapter 5

Repentance and Relationships: You Really Do Have to Say "I'm Sorry"

The heart is deceitful above all things and beyond cure. Who can understand it?

Jeremiah 17:9 (NIV)

Repent: intransitive verb—to feel regret or contrition, or to change one's mind

www.merriam-webster.com/dictionary/repent

In the tearjerker movie *Love Story,* the story is told of a young couple who falls in love and has a wonderful romance, only to end with the diagnosis of a terminal illness and eventual death on the part of the young woman. As the movie progresses, and they process grief and pain, she offers the famous words to her young lover, "Love means never having to say you are sorry." Although it was an effective line in that movie, it is not exactly helpful advice for the real world. The reality of most relationships is that love means having to say, "I'm sorry" over and over again. The biblical word for this is repentance. In Judeo-Christian understanding, saying "I'm sorry" and repentance are necessary for both forgiveness and intimacy. It is a very important part of intimate relationships.

Repentance is, however, far more than saying "I'm sorry." Without significant change, even sincere apologies mean little or nothing. Most people in intimate relationships become weary of hearing apologies without sincere change that follows. Repentance goes far beyond apology and is not the same as saying "I'm sorry." Repentance means a turnaround—a change of direction or an about-face. It refers to not only recognizing how we have hurt the other, but also staying committed to making serious personal change. Repentance is about taking personal responsibility to recognize how we have hurt someone, making a sincere apology, but then working on creating deep personal change to make sure we do not hurt them again. Repentance in this way of thinking is a difficult and painful process. No wonder so many people say "I know you said you are sorry, but you don't mean it." They are implying that they do not feel that other person gets the extent of the pain, and do not see a deep commitment to personal change. This type of repentance cannot happen without some deep introspection and self-awareness as described in the preceding chapter.

THE IMPORTANCE OF REPENTANCE

Why is repentance such a necessary ingredient in creating a mature, healthy marriage? The answer should be obvious. At least part of the reason is because most relationships have a predictable trajectory. They begin with a state of significant idealization. Most romances do not begin with the statement, "She is okay. She's got some good qualities, and some irritating ones, but I guess we can make a go of it." In reality, most relationships begin quite differently. In the early stages of falling in love, one sees his or her partner in idealized terms. They are close to perfect. They may have flaws, but their positive traits are what dominate our focus. Couples in this stage anticipate living happily ever after. They do not expect what follows. In fact, many couples who take the time and energy to pursue premarital counseling have difficulty getting much out of it since they cannot imagine seeing their partner as anything but ideal. Yet in the years that follow, the woman who is attracted to the carefree spontaneous man, who is so much fun to be with, never expected to be frustrated by his lack of seriousness, depth, and minimal work rate. The man married to a high-achieving career woman who initially admired her drive now sees her as "anal and uptight" and incapable of having fun. The woman who was attracted to the "bad boy" really hopes that he will calm down in marriage and becomes more critical of him as he continues to be himself. The man who marries the very nurturing woman, too often becomes enraged at her attempts to mother him. The examples are numerous, but no matter how many are listed, they all indicate the same problem: idealization eventually turns to disillusionment and pain. Disillusionment can easily then turn to attack and blame.

When marital disillusionment begins, relationships can move in two possible directions. One direction is to move toward a more mature love, while the other is toward blame and projection. Mature love requires individuals to have an ability to form a balanced picture of their partner. In this view strengths and weaknesses are both seen, and the partner is loved and accepted even with their flaws.

However, when things move in the negative direction, the very things that attracted couples in the beginning of the relationship are now problematic. Attack and blame increase, and acceptance decreases. In this process we see our partner's flaws, but none of our own problems or issues. In fact, too often we see more of our partner's flaws than their good points, and paradoxically, we see none of our own flaws. In the process, two pictures emerge: one of partner and one of self. The picture of partner becomes increasingly negative, while the picture of self is limited. In other words, all the blame is projected on the partner without any recognition of personal flaws, problems, or ways in which we are hurting the person we love. Therefore, the woman who is critical of her carefree husband for his low work ethic and laid-back lifestyle cannot recognize that her chronic overfunctioning and sometimes demanding style can help create the very thing that she is critical of. Conversely, the husband who is very critical of his wife for being no fun and too uptight does not recognize that his underfunctioning style leaves too much of the family pressure on his wife creating her "anal" style. Each is at least partially responsible for creating the very things they are critical of, and as a result, hurting their partner. The beginning of repentance is recognizing our own contribution to problems, and being committed to changing ourselves.

Blame and projection are the antithesis of acceptance and grace. Some of us, rather than accept who our partner is, complete with strengths and weaknesses, attack them for not being who we want them to be. In that sense, our blame is anger that the partner is not whom we want them to be; or as talked about in Chapter 3, anger that our idolatrous attempts to transform our partner have failed.

Most couples never dreamed that this would occur. They certainly never intended to hurt each other, yet they find themselves doing it over and over again. Sadly, they too often have difficulty realizing how they are hurting each other and are not aware of their own actions, and instead blame their partners for being oversensitive, misunderstanding, or unrealistic.

In the second couples therapy session, Sheila tearfully described Ted as insensitive and uncaring. "He just doesn't seem to care. My colleagues at work understand me better than my own husband. All he thinks about is himself, his job, and his running. He seems oblivious to my needs. He has no idea how much he has hurt me. It's like I'm living with a stranger." She hesitated and then added, "He thinks I'm superwoman without needs." Ted seemed stunned by these words. He thought of himself as a caring person. He certainly loved his wife, and so he was taken back to hear the pain in her voice. He had agreed to see a couples therapist thinking perhaps their marriage needed a slight tune-up, but had not realized the depth of pain his wife was feeling. Hearing Sheila's words he felt defensive and wanted to counterattack reminding her of some of her flaws. Yet some part of him knew he needed to listen and let Sheila express all that she was feeling. Repentance begins by forcing yourself to actually listen, not responding defensively, and really understanding the pain of your partner. It involves looking realistically at our contribution to our partner's pain and exploring our own capacity to hurt the people we love. This is very difficult work

REPENTANCE AND PROJECTION

Part of what makes this so difficult is our lack of recognition of what we have "projected" onto our partner. That was certainly part of Ted's problem. Having grown up with a very depressed and fragile mother, he was determined to find a strong woman who would not need taking care of. When he first met Sheila he was struck by her strength, her goals, and her quiet self-confidence. Without realizing it, he was also seeing her as someone without vulnerabilities and needs. The first few years of their marriage worked fine as they both pursued their own careers, enjoyed good friends, and wonderful vacations. Then they had children. Slowly their roles became unbalanced. Sheila was left with most of the responsibility for their three children while still holding much responsibility in her job as a head nurse in a very demanding hospital. At times she was exhausted and overwhelmed. However, Ted could never see it or more to the point would not let himself see it. When Sheila would become tired and sometimes depressed, he would tune out. He really didn't want to see her as vulnerable, and at times actually got angry when she seemed fragile. Unconsciously, this was reminding him of living with his very fragile mother. Without realizing it he expected Sheila to be highly competent and not vulnerable, which in turn caused him to not see her and to not understand that she was both competent and vulnerable. By only seeing part of her, he could tune out and just focus on his own needs and not even be aware of how much he was hurting her. It was no wonder that he was stunned by what Sheila shared in their marital therapy session. What is frightening in this case was how unconscious his "sin" was. He certainly never meant to hurt his wife. The last thing he ever consciously intended to do was create an unfair expectation of who Sheila should be that would block him from seeing what she needed from him. Ted was actually shocked when he saw the problem he had created.

The protestant reformer Martin Luther, defined sin as "the self curved inward," that is, the capacity to be self-absorbed and blind to the ways we hurt people around us. Sin, in Luther's definition, helps explain how we can be disconnected from what the needs are of the people around us. It explains how we can be so attached to what we think we need that we lose touch with or even be disconnected from what our partner needs. As a result the reality of the human condition is that we are often unaware of our capacity to hurt those we care about. The Old Testament prophet, Jeremiah, described this capacity for self-deception and lack of awareness: "the heart is deceitful above all things and beyond cure. Who can understand it?" (Jeremiah 17:9 [NIV]). Perhaps his words foreshadowed the psychoanalytic insight of Freud and others who described the ways in which human motivation is not as conscious as it seems. What does this concept of sin and unconscious motivation mean for couples? The implications are enormous. If people are not aware of their own issues, their own proclivities for selfishness, and the process of projection they are bound to hurt their partners on a regular basis, and too often, like Ted, not even be aware of the hurt they are causing. Intimacy is blocked when couples like Ted and Sheila relate to each other based on initial projected images, without letting go of those initial images, in favor of accepting the whole person. These projected images are based on what we think we need and therefore relate to our partners on the basis of that need, instead of seeing more clearly what our partners need.

In this regard, Sheila and Ted unfortunately typify many couples. They began their relationship with idealization and love, and now, a number of years later, are left feeling significant hurt and pain. Too often they are not even sure how they got there, since it was never their goal to hurt each other. Like Ted, many are stunned to hear how their partner feels hurt and misunderstood. Understanding how this hurt occurs is a crucial first step. Beginning the process of "repentance" is the next step but is always built on empathically understanding the pain of the other and becoming more aware of our own capacity to hurt those who are close to us.

SKILLS ARE PART OF REPENTANCE

Two significant skills are involved in this process of repentance. The first is the capacity for self-examination—the ability to honestly reflect on our capacity to cause pain even with the people we love. It begins with the question, "What did I contribute to this problem?" instead of rushing to blame our partner. That, of course, is a question that requires both courage and self-awareness.

The second skill is to listen empathically to what our partner describes without quickly moving toward defensiveness. Obviously this is far from easy. The dual skills of self-reflection and empathic listening without defensiveness are incredibly difficult. It is hard to see ourselves realistically, while at the same time listening to the pain expressed by our partners especially if we might have caused it. It is so much easier to move toward blame and defensiveness. The journey of introspection and empathy is far more difficult and requires the input of our partner. A spiritual life is a life lived in relationship. It is one thing to have a solitary spiritual practice; it is quite another to attempt to live out spirituality in relationship. It is one thing to talk about repentance; it is another to live it out relationally. If we believe our partner is key to our spiritual growth, we may be more apt to listen nondefensively to what he or she says about us and even see that as a spiritual opportunity.

Unfortunately, most people have great difficulty moving in this direction. Most people are convinced that their relational problems are the fault of their partner and have great difficulty seeing their own role in either the creation or maintaining of problems. As a result they continue the process of projection, and miss the opportunity for repentance and increased self-awareness. A New Testament story (John 8:1-11 [NIV]) illustrates the power of projection. In the story, a number of religious leaders have caught a woman in the act of committing adultery. They remind Jesus that the strict interpretation of the law is that she should be put to death by stoning. Jesus responds to the angry crowd, "Let him who is without sin cast the first stone," and the crowd slowly and quietly disperses. It takes great maturity to begin to see one's own role in a problem let alone the need for repentance and apology. It is so much more tempting to see all the problems as the fault of someone else, and then be angry at them. The angry crowd was able to project all their sins on this woman and then want to punish her accordingly. They certainly did not want to take responsibility for their own actions.

The capacity to see our own role in problems, not to mention our own sin, requires self-focus, which is referred to as differentiation (Bowen and Kerr, 1988). As discussed previously, differentiation is the ability to fully hold onto oneself nonreactively while maintaining emotional connection with one's partner. For Ted, this meant not reacting defensively to Sheila even when she was talking about the ways he had hurt her, holding onto his own desire to defend and counterattack, and actually listen carefully to what Sheila was saying. This level of differentiation is something that can grow over a lifetime. The higher the level of differentiation the easier it is to move toward repentance. The lower the level of differentiation the more projection and reactivity a relationship has. Part of the spiritual work of repentance is learning more about differentiation and learning more to hold onto our reactivity so that we can actually learn to hear what our partners are saying.

SIN

Part of moving forward toward better understanding of self and partner is to begin to understand sin. Sin is not a popular concept these days. In fact, most people would have difficulty connecting sin and relational problems. The focus within contemporary culture is on personal happiness, and as a result everything else becomes relative. What gets lost is the reality that there are many types of "sin" that get in the way of intimate relationships. Obviously, there are the large categories of relationship pain or sin such as adultery or addiction. These are easier to recognize. It is clear that when one cheats on one's partner one is hurting their partner. Addictions, such as alcoholism, are hurtful and destructive to people within intimate relationships. Domestic violence is devastating to the victim.

Unfortunately, it is easy to be self-righteous if none of these "big sins" are present. In the previously described New Testament story of the woman caught in adultery, part of the profound teaching of the story is that no one is without sin, and there are many types of sin and many ways in which we hurt one another: sins of self-absorption, the sins of taking our partner for granted, the sins of entitlement, the sins of not listening, the sins of misunderstanding, the list could easily go on and on.

Sin As a State of Being

Too often, sin is thought of as simply doing wrong things, and repentance is seen as confessing those specific acts of wrongdoing. Yet sin can also be seen as a state of being: a state of alienation or lack of wholeness. The reality is that we are all broken and that brokenness manifests in terms of problems in relationship to significant others, relationship to God, or even understanding self. As a result of this state of brokenness or alienation, it is easy to not even be aware of how we are hurting those we care about. When we are alienated from ourselves and from a sense of wholeness, then of course, we are bound to hurt those we love in a variety of ways.

Categories of Sin: Sins of Omission and Sins of Commission

There are two categories of "sin" in relationship. They have been referred to as sins of "omission" and sins of "commission." Sins of commission are the more "obvious sins," which describe specific acts. Sins of omission however are not so obvious. In either definition, both hurt and both can cause significant relational distance.

Sins of Omission

A good example of a relational "sin of omission" is empathic failure. If empathy is the ability to get inside the other, and know and feel what they are feeling, and be able to fully "get it" as explained in Chapter 2, then empathic failure is failing to get it. It is missing the other. Both empathic connection and empathic failure are fairly easy to recognize.

When, for example, you are trying to explain or describe a deep hurt or sadness, and you suddenly get the feeling that the person to whom you are describing it has no idea of what you are talking about, you have just experienced empathic failure. You can usually recognize this in increased frustration or agitation emerging from the fact that you feel totally misunderstood. Empathic connection is also easy to recognize. As discussed in Chapter 2, it is the feeling you get when you are deeply agitated or hurt, and share it with someone you care about and you feel totally understood. You can actually feel it in your body, as your body begins to relax. This level of empathy is an essential part of human relationships. In fact, some of the newer brain research suggests that it actually helps regulate the limbic system. This research suggests that the limbic system, the part of the brain that regulates emotion, is regulated by interpersonal empathic connection. It is no wonder we feel so much pain when we feel misunderstood!

Yet most people do not intentionally choose not to empathically listen to their partners. Most would not intentionally attempt to hurt their partners in any way. Yet if Luther is correct that sin is "the self turned inward," then it is easy for preoccupation with self to block our capacity to tune in empathically to our partners.

This, for most people, will be an ongoing struggle since staying empathically tuned in is hard work and for most does not come naturally. Our preoccupation with self and with our own needs, our own hurts, and our own agendas can make it difficult to empathically be tuned into our partners. The simple business of life, and of tiredness and pressures from multiple sources can cause us to sacrifice staying tuned in to our partners. Everything else can too easily take precedence. Ted never meant to lose contact with his wife Sheila. The last thing he ever wanted was for her to feel misunderstood and unimportant. Yet the business of work, family, and even his preoccupation with playing golf left his wife feeling significantly misunderstood. Certainly, this was an unintended failure of empathy. Change began for Ted in the recognition of his "sin" of empathic failure. It called for not only apologies but also long-term commitment to change and to different priorities. Staying empathically tuned into our partner means staying conscious, which in turn means making intentional decisions. For Ted "repentance" meant a real turnaround in terms of his priorities and where he stayed focused.

Sometimes, however, empathic failure is the result of other things. It is easy over the course of marriage to form a "picture" of our partner. "He is just controlling," or "She is so uptight," or "All that's important to him is his work," etc. We then relate to our partner through this picture. As a result we don't take the time to really understand our partner. We think our picture is correct: she really is just too uptight or he really is just controlling and so as a result we do not take the time to really understand who our partner really is. This was certainly the problem for Ted and Sheila. Ted had a picture of his wife that blocked his capacity to really know her. He believed that she was extremely competent and did not need much from him. He was of course partially right: she was competent in many ways but still needed him in many ways. She certainly needed to be understood. Like many, Ted's picture of his wife (which of course he never checked out with her) blocked him from really understanding his wife.

Finally, Ted, for a number of reasons, needed to hold onto this picture he had formed of his wife. Too often, lack of awareness of the baggage we bring into marriage block us from understanding what we project onto our partners. As explained earlier in this chapter, Ted needed to see his wife as strong and not "needy" like his fragile mother. As a result, this need, which he was not even aware of, blocked true empathy.

Failures of empathy are not usually intentional, which is why they are being referred to as sins of omission, but unintentional sin still has the same painful impact on relationships. Failures of empathy block us then from being attentive to the needs of our spouse and lead to many other frustrations and hurts. In this sense it is a "root sin." The inability to understand will result in a number of problems including problems in communication and listening, spending time in meaningful ways, and balancing responsibility. It is at the root of so many relationship problems.

The Sin of Entitlement

Failures to understand or to meet the needs of our spouse often come from a sense of entitlement, something we often do not take the time to think about. Entitlement is the assumption, often unconscious, that our needs deserve to be met. Often rooted in early childhood experiences, the person with entitlement issues believes that the world "owes" them. The child who was doted on, and became the prince or princess of the family, unconsciously expects the same type of treatment from his or her spouse. Paradoxically, people who grew up in a family where they felt invisible, and received little validation, too often expect that their spouse will help heal that wound by being there for them 24/7.

Of course, there are some gender considerations within this issue. Men have often been socialized to believe that their needs take priority, be it vocational needs or responsibilities. Ted, for example, took it for granted that he was "entitled" to play golf every weekend, and assumed that his wife would be responsible for the kids and the house in his absence. It never occurred to him to look at the lack of balance that this created in his marriage and the extra strain that it placed on his wife. He had difficulty even understanding Sheila's resentment. When she did complain he was quick to defensively explain all of the things he did around the house, all the while missing the sense of imbalance that his wife was describing.

Long-term entitlement creates deep resentment and distance. Too often couples are unable to get to the deeper issues of entitlement and the impact it has on their marriage. Only when the sense of entitlement is fully grasped can it lead to repentance and rebuilding.

Entitlement is also being included as a sin of "omission" because it is often not conscious. Unfortunately, most people are not even aware of the impact of their feelings of entitlement on the people in their lives. When they begin to better understand this impact the possibilities for improved empathy and partnership increase dramatically and powerful healing can take place.

The problem with sins of omission is that they are unconscious. For real healing to occur, they must be made conscious. A certain level of self-awareness is necessary in order for repentance and improved empathy to result.

The Sin of Internal Dialogue

People are often engaged in intense internal dialogue and are not even aware of its power. Although communication may look shutdown between people, the reality is that the communication is always going on internally. People carry on intense internal dialogue that they rarely share with their partner. Sheila, for example, often felt lonely and resentful. She often thought that Ted was insensitive and uncaring, and mostly focused on himself. She would have internal dialogues about this in her head and would think of all the things she wanted to say to Ted. Yet the dialogue stayed internal. So how is this a sin of omission? Some would argue that she was just attempting to be loving and not making Ted feel bad or creating more distance in the marriage. Yet her inability to be honest with Ted about her resentment and her internal dialogue resulted in increasing marital distance. Her internal resentment resulted in the loss of her libido. She was "never in the mood" much to Ted's frustration and often felt that sex was just one more pressure and responsibility. Her internal dialogue was in fact a type of dishonesty that made it more difficult for Ted to have some awareness of his entitlement and the lack of marital balance. The result was marital distance.

Ironically, this internal dialogue and reluctance to verbalize true feelings is a type of sin of omission that can have serious impact on a marriage. Like a failure of empathy, or a sense of entitlement, this type of sin of omission also needs repentance.

Taking Things for Granted

In the early part of relationships couples are excited to spend time together, and take delight in getting to know each other on deeper and deeper levels. The level of appreciation is high. Yet over time, it is surprising how little things go unacknowledged, and gradually things are taken for granted. Slowly, but surely, the excitement fades and that which was once special is now taken for granted, from the little special things to the larger issues. Slowly, but surely, too much is taken for granted and marital intimacy fades. Some would challenge seeing this as sin, but in reality, choosing not to focus on seeing the special things that one's partner does and neglecting to say thank you is a type of sin that erodes marital satisfaction. In the gospel story of the healing of the ten lepers, the account focuses on how only one returns to thank Jesus for the healing that he had received. The practice of gratitude is an essential part of a spiritual practice, and it is important to the nurturing of a quality marriage. Where we focus determines to some extent what we see. Therefore, when couples choose to focus more and talk more about what they appreciate, couple functioning is enhanced.

With all three of these relational sins of omission, repentance means first increased self-awareness where that which is often unconscious and internal becomes fully conscious. This is an essential first step. It is part of what the Old Testament Prophet Jeremiah meant when he said "The heart is deceitful above all things and beyond cure. Who can understand it?" (Jeremiah, 17:9 [NIV]). The human capacity for self-deception and lack of awareness can be significant. Moving toward increased awareness is the first step of repentance. Self-awareness is enhanced when we allow ourselves to listen nondefensively to the feedback of our partner and allow their critique to get in. This is very hard work. In the Old Testament story of King David (2 Samuel 11-12 [NIV]), the difficulty of self-awareness is clear. David sees Bathsheba bathing on her roof and has her brought to him. He gets her pregnant and then sends her husband Uriah to the front lines of battle where Uriah is killed. What is frightening in this story is not simply David's "sin." What is more disturbing is his self-deception. He continued to live as if there was no problem. Only when the Prophet Nathan confronts David with his sin does David actually repent. This powerful story unfortunately illustrates the problem with repentance. Too often, as Jeremiah reminds us, it is easy to practice self-deception.

Sins of Commission

Sins of commission are more obvious. They are the ways in which couples hurt each other in a variety of ways. These include the painful things that partners say in the heat of arguments, when they result in name-calling or deep personal attacks. These sins include insensitivity to meeting our partner's needs, especially when we know what our partners need and choose not to meet their needs.

Sins also include obvious behavioral issues such as infidelity. This category includes not only sexual affairs, but also emotional affairs when one becomes overly close to a colleague or co-worker, and share more with the person than with one's partner. Sins can also include addictions, financial mismanagement, or point-blank lies.

ACTION STEPS TOWARD REPENTANCE

Genuine repentance involves several important steps. These steps range from increased self-awareness to specific action steps. They can be summarized as follows:

1. *Self-awareness.* For many this is the hardest step. Self-awareness does not come easily. It is not a surprise that a spiritual life always involves a journey inward. John Calvin stated that the knowledge of God begins with knowledge of self. This increased self-awareness provides greater insight into the ways in which we often unintentionally hurt our partner, as the fruition of a spiritual journey is the awareness of our impact on others.
2. *Increased empathy through careful listening.* Awareness of how we have hurt those we love the most occurs when we listen carefully and nondefensively to their pain. For most this is extremely difficult. Listening is difficult enough, but listening without defending oneself takes enormous discipline.
3. *Acknowledge that we have done something wrong that has hurt our partner.* The wronged person needs to hear a clear statement that his or her partner understands that they have caused deep hurt and pain. Unless the wronged partner believes that his or her partner really understands how they have hurt them, it will be difficult to move forward and make repair.

Following this acknowledgment, there must be a sincere confession and asking for forgiveness. This may need to be repeated several times.

Following this "confession" there must be a clear plan to not repeat the same hurtful action. Talk is cheap, and too often partners are reluctant to believe that there will be real and long-lasting change. Remember, repentance means an about-face; a significant lifestyle change. Confession is enhanced when the partner demonstrates not only a commitment to change, but also provides a clear plan for how this change will take place.

Part of this plan may involve compensation or restitution. Does that mean offering some type of financial payout to one's spouse? Not at all. However, some restitution is always in order. For example, one husband who had been unfaithful told his wife that he would do whatever it took to rebuild her trust and was literally willing to do whatever she requested.

Following this comes a sincere request for forgiveness with the understanding that this request might have to be repeated several times and backed up by action.

Finally, repentance involves a determination to act differently on a consistent basis, even when one's partner is not ready to grant forgiveness. This involves the capacity to "hold onto oneself" to not become reactive and to not give up too quickly. Genuine repentance means holding onto a desire to change whether or not your partner agrees; repentance demands both self-awareness and the capacity for differentiation. It is the ability to see your role in hurting your partner, "confess" to your partner how much you realize they have been hurt, but then hold onto your reactivity if they do not easily appreciate the act of repentance. It means holding on to oneself and continuing to talk about it with your partner.

Chapter 6

Intimacy and Forgiveness

Forgive "To stop feeling angry or resentful toward someone for an offense, flaw, or mistake." To cancel a debt.

Brown, 1971

Lord, if another member of the church sins against me, how often should I forgive? As many as seven times? Jesus said to him, "Not seven times, but I tell you, seventy-seven times.

Matthew 18:21, 22 (NIV)

The gospel is full of wonderful stories of forgiveness. Jesus forgives the woman who is caught in adultery, despite the angry mob who wants her to be punished. Zaccheus, the tax collector, is forgiven and finds acceptance and Jesus even goes to his house. In the New Testament, story after story portrays broken people finding forgiveness and acceptance. Many of these stories point to God's gracious forgiveness to those who deserve it least. These stories contain universal themes. First, they reveal that all are broken and have sinned ("Let him who is without sin cast the first stone"). Second, forgiveness comes from outside of the self. Finally, it is not deserved. The New Testament refers to it as grace: God's total and unconditional acceptance. The story of the woman caught in adultery is illustrative. Jesus condemns not her, but all those who wanted to punish her for not recognizing their own "sin" or brokenness. Psychology refers to this as *projection:* they projected their sin onto her and then wanted to stone her for it as opposed to accepting their own sin. No one in the story deserved forgiveness or could offer it to themselves; the woman that

Jesus encounters was trapped in her own dysfunctional lifestyle. Jesus takes the initiative to offer forgiveness and a new way of life. Finally, the story profoundly illustrates God's love, acceptance, and grace for all.

It is one thing to study these forgiveness stories in Sunday school and listen to sermons that explore the nature of God's love and forgiveness. It is at times even emotionally moving to celebrate God's forgiveness through one of the rituals of the church such as communion. However, it is one thing to understand forgiveness; it is another to practice it within the context of marriage. It is one thing to reflect on the biblical stories of forgiveness and explore what they mean; it is another to practice forgiveness when hurt by the person you love.

Marriage is full of irritations, small hurts, misunderstandings, and major wounds. There are no shortage of opportunities for saying "I'm sorry" and for repentance, and multiple opportunities for repentance. Theoretically, to forgive and forget does not sound that difficult. On the surface one person apologizes and the other accepts the apology and then moves forward. It sounds simple. Yet anyone who has been married for a long time, or has listened to couples in the midst of their intense struggles, knows how complicated forgiveness really is. Most would say it is an essential part of living in relationship and certainly an essential part of living a spiritual life. Yet, for most, it remains tremendously difficult for a number of reasons.

Forgiveness begins with the victimized one recognizing that an actual injustice was committed against them. Having recognized the injustice, and confronted the person who hurt them, forgiveness means the victim chooses willingly to respond with mercy as opposed to retribution. On the surface it sounds like a three step process: recognize the injustice, confront the person with it, and then respond with mercy. However, in so doing, there is much to process in this definition since it taps into a complex array of human emotions. It taps into hurt, anger, betrayal, sometimes disorientation, and quite often—intense vulnerability. It is one of the most complicated human interactions.

Maria and Tony are a good example of the complexity.

During the early years of their marriage Tony, by his own admission, was immature and self-centered. He was irresponsible with money, partied hard with his old college friends, and left too much of the responsibility to his wife, Maria. He explained that he needed at least one night out "with the boys" and could not understand why Maria was so upset about the way he would drive home after having too much drink. He referred to her concern as nagging, and told Maria not to mother him. His solution to the problem was to suggest she go out more with her friends.

As their marriage moved forward, Maria, by necessity, took on more and more responsibility. She took care of the finances, the house, and their two children, and often sarcastically referred to Tony as her most difficult child. At the same time she learned that it was never helpful to confront Tony because he became intensely angry and defensive, and so she learned to become more and more overresponsible, while internally simmering with resentment. Not surprisingly, she lost interest in sexual intimacy as she became more and more emotionally distant from her husband over the years. Other than complaining that they didn't have sex often enough, Tony never seemed to notice how emotionally distant his wife was and constantly criticized her as being his mother.

After twelve years of marriage, Tony's father died suddenly. His death occurred just as he retired ending dreams of a wonderful retirement life full of travel and golf. Several months after the funeral, Tony started to become depressed. His "good ole boy" personality began to change. He began to withdraw from his friends and think more about what he wanted out of life. Life seemed absurd. His father had worked hard and saved for retirement. He was well loved by all his friends and was in good health. Tony could not make sense of it. He made an appointment to talk to his physician about his loss of energy and lack of appetite. His doctor suggested that he start seeing someone for psychotherapy. To his wife's surprise, he not only started therapy but also stuck with it. At the same time he became more actively engaged with his faith community and joined a men's group. Maria was shocked; she had never seen the introspective side of Tony before. She of course wondered if this would last or was just a passing fad. Tony, however, began to realize his sense of entitlement and how it had impacted Maria for the twelve years of their marriage; he actually began to feel guilty. The men's group suggested he make a careful apology to his wife.

Tony wanted to practice the principles of repentance outlined in Chapter 5, and so made an emotional apology to his wife Maria. He acknowledged that he was beginning to understand how his selfishness and immaturity had impacted her, and actually described in some detail the ways he had been a poor husband and asked for her forgiveness. Maria was shocked. She had quietly hoped that his newly found introspection would bring insight, but never expected that this is where it would go.

So far, so good. The problem is that Tony's apology has put the ball in Maria's hands. What will it mean for her to forgive Tony? What does she do with twelve years of resentment? Will she now be able to trust Tony in a way that will strengthen their intimacy? If she forgives him, and allows herself to trust him in new ways, will he disappoint her again? These are some of the complicated aspects of relational forgiveness. Maria has to not only decide what to do with all of the resentment, but also whether she can let go of wanting to exact some punishment for all that she has lost during the partying years because of Tony. She still resented being referred to as his mother as he went out for beer with his friends. Finally, she must decide whether she can allow herself to begin to be both vulnerable and intimate with her husband.

If she forgives, she may also have to confront her overfunctioning role within the marriage and begin to let it go in order to create balance. Although on the one hand this is what she has insisted she has always wanted, giving up the control that comes with her role is not simple. Forgiveness in this case can also lead to unbalancing the marriage and illustrates how complicated it can be.

Tim and Paula present another forgiveness dilemma. Fifteen years into the marriage, Tim became suspicious that Paula was having an affair with a colleague at work. He confronted Paula with his suspicions, but she indignantly stated that she was not having an affair and was just friends with one of her male co-workers, and angrily accused Tim of not trusting her. However, Tim had difficulty trusting that he was really getting the truth. He eventually looked at Paula's e-mail account and found the evidence that Paula was actually having an affair that had been going on for the past seven months. He discovered that some of her business trips were actually with the male co-worker that he had been suspicious of.

Tim confronted Paula with the evidence. After initially saying that it was not an affair, she finally broke down and tearfully told Tim the truth. She agreed to end the affair and enter marriage counseling. She begged Tim not to leave her and resolved to anything necessary to rebuild trust. After several months of couples therapy Paula asked Tim to forgive her and to trust her again.

Tim was torn. He wanted to forgive her, but at the same time could not get the images of his wife being with another man out of his head. He could not help but remember that she had lied to him before, and sometimes even wondered if she still had contact with her lover. He was terrified that she would do it again, and didn't know how he would ever trust again or be able to offer forgiveness. For Tim to forgive, he needed first to wrestle with whether he will exact vengeance—the "eye for an eye" concept. He wondered about having an affair himself as a type of payback. He angrily confronted Paula with questions about how she would react if he had an affair. He also realized on some level that if he forgave her and "canceled the debt" he might be letting her off the hook. After all, didn't she owe him something? Shouldn't there be some type of payback? Certainly to "cancel the debt" at this point wasn't fair. Many people, like Tim, really believe that they are entitled to some payback from their partner besides just rebuilding trust. Shouldn't their partner "make it up to them" somehow? That is the practical outworking of the issue of forgiveness and a debt. To forgive the debt is to symbolically become poorer and to lose some leverage. Tim was well aware of this. Even more, to forgive would give up his right to keep hammering his wife with what she had done, but also to move back to a more emotionally intimate marriage. Doing so would make him more vulnerable.

Finally, to complete the process, Tim would have to accept that his actions may have contributed to the affair. Deep down, he knew that he had not been emotionally present to Paula during some very difficult times in her life. On a good day he could even see how his lack of emotional availability could have left her vulnerable and needy. However, beginning to understand that, and eventually sharing it with Paula was another issue. Sharing these feelings is a final step of forgiveness, and of letting go. Done well it will lead to deeper levels of intimacy, but at the same time it is difficult and frightening work.

Both cases demonstrate the complexity of forgiveness. Both raise multiple questions that have no easy answers. Forgiveness relates to rebuilding trust, allowing closeness and renewed intimacy, agreeing to not hold the "sin" against the partner, and dealing with powerful memories. Forgiveness is far from easy. It is always risky. Without it, however, intimacy cannot move forward; forgiveness always feels risky.

FORGIVENESS AS A LEAP OF FAITH

The concept of faith in religion suggests that deep spirituality does not come simply through rational evaluation, or by study, or by learning certain key propositions of faith. Rather spirituality suggests that at some point there is a "leap of faith." Kierkegaard (1983) reminds us that the "real truth" is the subjective truth, not objective truth. Objective truth is arrived at through rational investigation; subjective truth is arrived at differently. It requires a leap of faith and a commitment. In the same way, forgiveness is a "leap of faith" since the outcome is not guaranteed; there is simply no way to make it objective. In many ways offering forgiveness makes one even more vulnerable. It means letting go of one's anger and giving up the right to exact revenge. Forgiveness literally means canceling a debt and therefore giving up the right to retribution or punishment and the satisfaction that might come from that. However, in so doing, the victim is giving up something, and they often experience a loss of power. In contrast holding onto the grudge or the debt keeps the victim somewhat empowered. As long as they hold the grudge, they maintain some level of control and power which lets them feel a little safer, and can continue to demand some type of reparation. Both Maria and Tony had to struggle with this in powerful ways. Maria struggled with the question of whether she was letting Tony off the hook too easily. After all, she had been overresponsible, exhausted, and lonely for many years, while Tony was off having a great time. She resented that everybody thought her husband was the life of the party and loved being with him, while she was afraid that their friends saw her as too boring and serious. She wondered if she was giving in too easily. Shouldn't Tony have to prove something to her? How was she to know if this was just a fad and that once he felt better she would be on her own again. She already saw him beginning to spend a lot of time with the men in his support group. For Maria "canceling the debt" was complicated.

Obviously for Tim the issue was equally complicated. The pain of an affair is powerful and can easily feel like the deepest violation possible. How could he "cancel the debt"? How would he know when there had been enough payback? How could he possibly even consider rebuilding trust?

Holding off on giving forgiveness and exacting payment on the debt creates a sense of power. It causes the person that hurt you to continue to suffer and this does provide at least some satisfaction. This perceived power in return allows one to avoid feeling the deep anxiety of vulnerability. It is actually a defense against deeper pain. Forgiveness is threatening because it is the letting go of this perceived power. In so doing, it opens up the possibility of deeper intimacy, deeper trust, and deeper hurt. If one lets go of anger, forgives, and begins to trust again, then future betrayal hurts even more. That is the problem of forgiveness as a leap of faith. The leap is the hope (but not the guarantee) that one will not be hurt again.

THE STEPS OF FORGIVENESS

If forgiveness is thought of as a series of steps—the first one is the easiest. The first step is identifying the hurt or offense. The offense can be large or small. It can involve betrayal such as an affair. A betrayal involving finances may occur when one person spends large amounts of money, hiding it from their partner. The offense can be the result of one person being forced to overfunction while the other does not carry the weight in terms of household responsibilities or finances for an extended period of time. Other offenses can be the multiple ways in which people hurt each other ranging from not listening and failures of empathy, to harsh criticism, to name-calling, to ignoring a partner's need, as well as many other examples. It is certainly not hard to come up with multiple varieties of offenses, and for most it is not difficult to recognize hurt.

Step One: Confrontation

The first step in moving toward forgiveness is confrontation. For those who are conflict avoidant, this is not easy. The conflict-avoidant person always wants to make peace and avoid conflicts, tends to bury hurt, and wants to avoid confronting the other person. Unfortunately, they pay a powerful price for this avoidance. Their resentment level will continue to grow, and they will become more and more emotionally distant. They may become depressed or begin to have somatic issues such as headaches or backaches. They may experience a loss of sexual desire, since often the loss of sexual desire is the result of simmering resentment and anger. Forgiveness is made impossible because there is no confronting of the offense.

For others, confronting the offense is not difficult. They have no difficulty confronting their partner, at least initially. In fact they are more than ready to confront their partner, and remind them over and over again of how they have been hurt. However, even for those unafraid of confrontation, things rarely go well in the first conversation about the issue. For both Maria and Tim, their first confronting of the offense did not go well. In order to move toward intimacy and practice forgiveness, it is necessary to be assertive and consistent about making sure the other does actually get it.

The next step is complicated. Once the offense has been confronted, the wounded partner must make a decision as to what to do next. There are a number of options: they can keep reminding their partner of all the ways they have hurt them, they can distance emotionally and physically, or they can even hold out for their partner to prove something to them. Sometimes they even need space physically and as a result choose to live separately for a period of time.

Certainly, their partner's response is an important factor in deciding what to do next. When Maria first confronted Tony early in their marriage about the imbalance in their relationship, he accused her of trying to be his mother. When she tried to problem solve with him about how they could share more of the roles, he made a few token efforts, and then slid back to his old way of doing things. Maria slowly stopped bringing up the issue, and made the best of things, while she became more distant and resentful. In this example, Maria was not in a position to move toward forgiveness since her husband was giving her nothing to work with. It is very difficult to move forward with the process of forgiveness when there is no acknowledgment from the partner that they actually get it, and take some responsibility for the pain.

Step Two: Forgiveness and Canceling the Debt

Step two is much harder. Assuming that one has been able to "confront the offense," that one's partner has actually heard it, taken responsibility, and actually asked for forgiveness, then the issue of "canceling the debt" becomes the issue to work through. This is very difficult work depending on the severity of the offense. It is certainly easier to "cancel debts" for small offenses. These tend to be fairly simple interactions for healthy couples. One hurts the other by being late for dinner and not calling, or by being inattentive and not listening. The offense is recognized: one person apologizes after realizing his or her insensitivity and often the other can forgive and "cancel the debt." However, even that simple interaction is dependent on several variables. The partner expressing the hurt needs to understand that their partner actually gets it, and is not just making an apology to end the conflict. Too often one partner says "but I said I was sorry," to which the other responds "but you don't even understand what you are apologizing for!" This is the case of the infamously insincere apology that says "I'm sorry for whatever I did that you think hurt you." Obviously, this will not be helpful.

For this transaction to work, two things are critical. First, there must be empathy and deep understanding of what the offense really is, and then a profound commitment to really make a change (true repentance). If these two issues are present it is easier to forgive. Even then larger offenses, such as those in the case examples, make letting go of the debt very complicated. In both case studies, both Maria and Tim believed that their partners understood the extent of their hurt. They even felt a degree of empathy, but initially it was not enough to be helpful. Both still needed to hold onto the anger in order to feel safe and not become too vulnerable. Both had felt deep hurt, betrayal, and depression as a result of their partner's actions. Canceling the debt in this case is heavily dependent on how the partner responds. This level of deep hurt can heal only as one experiences the accurate empathy of the partner. If one senses that one's partner minimizes the pain, or suggests "Didn't we already talk about this? Why do we have to re-hash it one more time?" then it is much more difficult to forgive since the partner who has been hurt believes that his or her pain is being minimized and not taken seriously. It is only when one senses that one's partner empathically understands the extent of the pain that one really begins to let go. When Tim realized that his wife not only un-derstood the depth of his pain but also was in deep pain herself he was able to begin moving forward. During a therapy session, she began to cry softly as Tim described his own depression and loss of deep trust. As the therapist asked her to describe to Tim what she was feeling, she tearfully said, "I just can't believe I've done this to Tim. He has always been there for me, and now I've hurt the person I love the most. I never believed I was the type of person who could create such pain. I do not deserve his love, and I'm not sure I can ever forgive my-self." As she put her head down and sobbed, Tim began to soften. He realized in that moment that his wife not only understood how deeply she had hurt him, but was also feeling deep pain herself in knowing she was capable of that type of hurt and betrayal. This allowed Tim to begin to slowly be able to cancel the debt. He knew at that point that to keep punishing her emotionally for the affair was not going to help either of them.

Canceling the debt of serious relationship injuries requires both deep empathy as well as the ability to know that one's partner is suf-fering with you. Without this, it is difficult to move to the next step.

People who can move toward forgiveness and let go of the right to keep "punishing" their partner are also able to feel empathy toward their partner in a way that allows them to better understand how their partner hurt them. As difficult as it is, they may realize that they are also part of the problem. This is part of spiritual growth. The "bad news" of the gospel, is that we are all broken. There really are no saints or sinners. The reality of life is that when we look within, we are not only flawed but also very capable of hurting others. The reality of a spiritual journey is the recognition that there are few "innocent victims." It is perhaps part of what the New Testament writer meant in saying "For all have sinned and fall short. . . ." This is a difficult reality to accept in the practice of forgiveness. It certainly cannot be rushed, and when the guilty partner states it as an accusation it is next to impossible. For example, when one partner says "If you hadn't ignored me for all these years, I might never have had this affair," the conflict will inevitably escalate, and forgiveness will not be the result. The partner must realize his or her part in the problem as a result of careful introspection and without pressure from the partner who has committed the offense.

At the same time, without this layer of complicated empathy, genuine forgiveness is not likely. Empathy needs to move in both directions here. Offending partners must be able to communicate effectively that they really understand the impact of their actions on their partner. They must be able to communicate that they really get it, without falling into defensiveness or making excuses for their actions. However, empathy must also move in the opposite direction. It means the "victim" is able to find some way of understanding the actions of their partner. While not at all excusing those actions, they must find some way of resonating with those actions, meaning they will find some way of recognizing their own problems and ways that they have also hurt their partner. They will move away from believing that they are the "suffering saint" living with a "sinner." This is always extremely difficult, and powerfully emotional work, but inevitably it results in a stronger movement toward forgiveness.

Step Three: Forgiveness and Intimacy

Of all the steps involved in forgiving this one is inevitably the most complicated and the most risky. It is never easy to forgive the debt and slowly release the emotional power that was the interest accruing on the debt. It is quite another issue to decide whether to move toward intimacy. Many relationships are unable to move to this level. They may be able to let go of the debt, but are unable to take the risk of allowing intimacy, and the potential for hurt and vulnerability begin to emerge. When this occurs, deep levels of intimacy are not possible.

For deep levels of intimacy to be possible, one must be open, trusting, and vulnerable.

A very difficult decision is part of this step. The injured person must attempt to decide whether he or she is able to move back into an intimate relationship with the person who hurt them. Sometimes the answer is clearly no.

Helen was able leave her husband after many year of domestic violence. For years she had felt trapped in a violent and abusive relationship. Finally, after very difficult work, she found a way to leave and live on her own. After much therapy she began to realize that to move on with her life, she needed to forgive her ex-husband but that raised many red flags for her. Did that mean that if he apologized and she forgave him, she must go back into the relationship? Clearly not! Forgiveness must be thought of as progressive levels with complicated decisions made at each level. Helen struggled whether to even forgive the debt. However, she realized that to continue to harbor resentment and anger, with fantasies of revenge, would only keep her stuck and unable to move on with her life. She was aware that the pain of that abuse was always in the "rearview mirror" of her mind and was keeping her overly cautious in her new relationship. Slowly, she was able to see her ex-husband as a victim of abuse himself and begin to see him in a softer light. She was able to slowly forgive him for the pain and agony that he had put her through. However, she was equally clear that she would never reconcile with him, and probably never take the risk of being alone with him to even talk this through. She forgave, but was not willing to move forward with an intimate relationship.

Many adult children who have suffered through physical or sexual abuse make this decision. To never forgive is sometimes to remain a victim and not move forward. At the same time building an intimate relationship with someone who was that abusive is all but impossible. So many adults, like Helen, decide to forgive, may even "cancel the debt," but can never move toward any type of intimacy. For them, forgiveness is still a spiritual opportunity, but does not require moving toward the next level of intimacy.

For many of the couples I work with, this is a painful and complicated decision. Does Rita forgive Stephen after realizing that he has had numerous affairs throughout their twenty-year marriage? Does Claudia forgive and become intimate again with Peter after recognizing that his gambling addiction has threatened their family finances? These and many other examples illustrate the complexity of the final stage. For some the spiritual practice of forgiveness means canceling the debt and rebuilding intimacy. For others it means that genuine for-giveness may be offered, but the potential for long-term intimacy will never be possible.

For couples, these are very difficult decisions and require wisdom and courage. Being clear about the hurt is the first step. Deciding how to "cancel the debt" is the next step, but moving toward intimacy is the last and final step and certainly the most difficult. It is a step that must be thought through, but one that can fundamentally change a re-lationship as well as the people in it.

It is a step that is again contingent on the levels of differentiation for each partner; that is how well one can hold onto oneself non-reactively, but at the same time be clear about what one needs. Cou-ples who do this avoid some of the classic extremes. For one group of couples, forgiveness is given quickly. They will certainly achieve a conflict-free relationship that is in the end polite, friendly, but cer-tainly not intimate. On the other extreme are those who can never let their partner forget how they were hurt and keep using that hurt as a psychological club.

Couples who are working at higher levels of differentiation talk through the hurtful issues until both feel completely understood. They do not bury the issue prematurely. Their goal in communication is certainly not to beat the issue to death, but to make sure that the "vic-tim" feels empathically understood. The conversation cannot end un-til the injured parties feel like their pain is completely understood but that is not enough. The injured party must be assertive enough to set some boundaries that will help rebuild trust. Examples might include trust-building exercises that allow the betrayed person to ask for whatever will help them rebuild trust, or might involve a shift in how finances are handled so that there is no risk in more gambling debt. There are many examples of setting boundaries that allow intimacy to move forward.

Intimacy cannot be achieved without clear boundaries, and so part of the work of differentiation is to not only be empathically under-stood, but also to put appropriate boundaries in place that create a sense of safety. From this safe place intimacy can slowly be rebuilt. Without those boundaries and requests being made, victims can feel a sense of shame that they took no action despite the significant hurt that they experienced. This can be an additional block to intimacy.

When the steps are taken, and boundaries put in place, there is great potential for intimacy. Part of the working through is the potential for each to be better understood, for their vulnerabilities to be made clearer, and for the potential to rediscover more of each other.

This, however, is the result of very hard work combining both repentance and forgiveness, and drawing on each person's capacity for differentiation. There are no shortcuts. It is a slow, painful process that can produce great potential for intimacy and spiritual growth.

SUMMARY OF STEPS TOWARD FORGIVENESS

- Explore the symptoms of unresolved hurt. Is there distance, lack of passion, unresolved anger? If so, there will be significant distance in the relationship.
- Begin to attempt to put into words the hurt that is unresolved. Make a commitment to stay with the conversation until you begin to feel understood. This involves making a commitment to not become reactive and to not get derailed into other issues in the relationship.
- Consider whether your partner understands the nature of your hurt, and whether they are truly sorry. This then raises the question of whether you can forgive in the sense of not "holding" the offense over your partner.
- Begin to wrestle with canceling the debt by letting go of the emotional power of the hurt. Often talking to a therapist or spiritual guide is a helpful part of this process.
- Finally, recognize the profound spiritual truth that no one is perfect, and that "all have sinned." As difficult as it can be, recognizing and owning your own contribution and capacity to hurt can be very helpful.

Chapter 7

Salvation, Marriage, and Grace

Amazing Grace, how sweet the sound that saved a wretch like me. I once was lost, but now I'm found, was blind, but now I see.

Amazing Grace

Grace, it's the name for a girl. It's also a thought that changed the world.

Bono, U2

For it is by Grace you have been saved, through faith—and this not from yourselves, it is the gift of God. . . .

Ephesians 2:8, 9 (NIV)

There are many fantasies about marriage. The magic of the wedding ceremony speaks to the powerful expectations that each partner has: expectations that are perhaps so profound that they cannot even be put into words. These expectations, or what might be called marital myths, may include fantasies for a type of oneness ("the two shall become one") where two marital partners have such a close relationship they share everything in common and become "soul mates." Another common marital myth suggests that in marriage there is the potential for being completed by one's spouse ("she's my better half"). In this scenario what is missing in us we find in our partner, such as the carefree woman marrying the overresponsible man, or the introvert marrying the extrovert. Still another myth suggests the potential that marriage has for healing of old injuries and wounds created early in life in our original families; someone who will make up for the deprivations and disappointments of childhood. Some couples unconsciously combine all of these myths expecting a perfect life together. Saying "I do" is a way of assenting to some combination of these myths that hopefully will lead to paradise. Unfortunately these powerful expectations or marital myths are usually unconscious, and are rarely verbalized, let alone carefully negotiated by both partners before entering into marriage.

Implicit within all of this is perhaps a longing that can't be put into words for most who marry. Marriage can represent a longing for connectedness, for a sense of wholeness, for an end to aloneness or loneliness or even despair. After all, who has not felt alone in the world, and felt acute existential angst as the result of that sense of isolation? Who has not longed to be with someone in such a way that that profound aloneness, anxiety, and even depression will be healed? The expectations for finding some type of "salvation or wholeness" in marriage are enormous and rarely put into words.

The reality is most people are disappointed. What most people had unconsciously hoped for in marriage is a type of "salvation" or a making whole that will rescue them, complete them, and launch them on a new life together. It is no wonder that when things are going well, some refer to marriage as heaven, while when things are going badly it feels like hell.

SALVATION AS A RELIGIOUS CONCEPT

For most religions the concept of salvation is central. It is the end result of faithfully following the teachings of one's religion, or of the church, leading to finding acceptance by God. The result is the reward of eternal life in heaven, and the end of pain and suffering.

Salvation as a religious concept begins with the concept of sin or separation. In Judeo-Christian teachings, sin is not simply understood as "sinful acts" (such as lying, stealing, committing adultery, etc.), but it is rather a profound separation that occurs on several levels. In the Genesis narrative the story describes Adam and Eve in an idyllic state of a perfect relationship. In the midst of this perfection they eat of the forbidden fruit, resulting in a "fall." This separation manifests in three ways: they are separated from God, from each other, and even from themselves. Their separation from God is reflected in the description of them hiding from God in the bushes, afraid to be seen or to be in relationship. They are separated from each other, as they begin to argue and to blame each other for what has gone wrong ("It wasn't my fault, it was Eve"). They are separated from the self that they were created to be. Suddenly they are aware of guilt and shame, and want to hide and not be seen by God or by each other. What is significant in the story is not their particular sin (eating the forbidden fruit), but their sense of separation. They are alienated from their true selves, the self they were created to be, from each other (the type of relationship they were created to live in), and from God, defined in Acts 17:28 (NIV): "'For in him we live and move and have our being.' As some of your own poets have said, 'We are his offspring.'"

Understood in these terms, their longing for salvation is the longing for wholeness. Feeling separate from this they begin to blame, and they experience both guilt and shame in the story losing connection to themselves, to each other, and to God. Their quest for salvation then is about being reconciled to God, to each other, and even to themselves. Kierkegaard (1983) expands this concept in his classic book *The Sickness unto Death,* by suggesting that when one is not the self that they were created to be, they are living a "false self" existence, which in turn will lead to increased anxiety and eventually to despair. He argues that separation results in trying hard to be a self (usually a false self), which in the end creates distance, anxiety, and even despair.

Salvation then is not so much about earning eternal life as a reward for finding the right relationship with God, but rather it is about being restored to the self one was meant to be. It is about being accepted just for who you are, and about restoration to wholeness. While not minimizing traditional religious thinking relating salvation to teachings about heaven and hell and an afterlife, the understanding of salvation being discussed here focuses on the need for wholeness, restoration, and the healing of separation. Too many people describe the agony of feeling separated from their partner, separation at time from themselves, as well as from any type of profound meaning. Many hope that marriage will help restore them to wholeness and to a type of salvation. How often have couple therapists heard one partner say, "I miss the man I married?" This usually means that the original person seems to have vanished as he has tried so hard to be successful, or has become more shut down by depression or shame.

SALVATION AND MARRIAGE

Andrew had grown up in a fundamentalist family. His social life revolved around the Baptist Church attended by his family, which in turn consumed large amounts of his time. He attended Sunday school, morning services, evening services, youth meetings, as well as prayer meetings. He often felt isolated from his friends at school, since his family insisted on him being part of all church activities and forbade him from going to school dances, and were deeply suspicious of his school friends. His parents were rigid and angry in their religious ideology. They were extremely critical of his friends and of all nonbelievers. His father was impossible to get close to. He was an angry man, who was both verbally and physically abusive. If confronted, he could fly into a rage and lash out at whoever was there. Andrew could never reconcile the religious views espoused by his father, and his father's constant anger and controlling behavior.

As a result, he began to distance emotionally, and grew up isolated and alone, resenting his family and their religious zeal. He was tired of always being evaluated and criticized by the standards of his parent's religion. Because he tended to be the rebel in the family, he never received validation from his parents. Worse than that, he was constantly criticized because of his doubts and told by his parents that they would keep praying for him. They were suspicious of everything he did, and interpreted all of his questions as challenges to them, their faith, and even to God. His father's oft-repeated line to Andrew was "When will you stop rebelling against God?" They could not understand his doubt, his questions, or his anger. As a result of his questioning he received little or no mirroring from his family, except in so far as he did something special in the church.

The result of all of this caused Andrew to deeply distrust himself. While he could be outspoken and critical, he often doubted himself since he received so little validation from his family. On the one hand, he did not fit into his family, but on the other was not allowed to have a social life apart from his church. He was uneasy socially and constantly felt that no one had ever given him the "guidebook" that explains how life is supposed to be lived. All he knew was the suffocating rules of the church that his parents were part of which did not help him negotiate life in the real world.

He hoped that when he fell in love with Kim that he would no longer be alone, and that he would finally be understood and validated, and when they first fell in love that is what they experienced. In the early stages of their relationship, he remembered feeling so in love that he felt as if he was high. He would fall asleep looking forward to what they would do the next day. As their relationship became sexual it felt intoxicating, especially since his family had not been at all demonstrative physically. He could not get enough of Kim in every sense of the word. However, as time moved forward, and after they had been married for several years, things began to shift. One of the first shifts occurred whenever he did not feel understood by Kim. When this occurred he would become deeply depressed and angry, and then withdraw, often feeling as alone as he did as a child.

The "salvation" that Andrew hoped for was not going to be easy. Yet his marriage represented an opportunity for profound spiritual work that might bring him closer to what he hoped for. On some level, Andrew knew what he was doing when he married Kim. She was certainly not someone who was going to suffocate him like his parents and had lots of friends. She was not overly emotional and critical like his mother. So far, so good. Yet her lack of emotion sometimes felt wounding and at times Andrew would feel like she did not get it. In addition, her extroverted style sometimes left him feeling a bit abandoned. He sometimes interpreted her going out with friends as "abandoning" him and resented it. At the same time, he knew how ridiculous that sounded, and so kept that feeling inside and never shared it with his wife. The result, however, was distance and resentment, and much of the time his wife did not even know why he was so distant and remote.

This was not the marriage that Andrew had hoped for. It certainly was not what his wife had hoped for either. Kim had grown up with a father with bipolar disorder, and a mother who seemed overwhelmed constantly and would withdraw to her bedroom to sleep, often leaving her children to fend for themselves. To escape her home, Kim found safety in friendship and spent much of her adolescence staying with friends at their homes. She learned to stay level and nonemotional, hoping to bring some calm to a very chaotic home. The last thing she wanted was to add to the emotional reactivity. Dinner times were a nightmare because she never knew when her father was going to explode, especially if he had been self-medicating with alcohol. Expressing emotion or a strong opinion during these dinner conversations was a great way to get her father going, which was never pleasant. Her two defenses were her extroverted ability to connect with friends and her ability to regulate her own emotion so that she never "rocked the boat." Not surprising, despite her extroverted characteristics, her family did not know anything about her. They did not know her friends, her interests, and certainly never knew what she was feeling. She picked her own college with little help from her parents and saw very little of them during the years she was away. Not surprisingly, she had many friends, including many boyfriends, but none that ever got to know her deeply. She had a great time going out, but was always left with a nagging sense that no one really knew her.

When she met Andrew that began to change. She was attracted to his introspective abilities, his interest in spirituality, his gentleness, and his ability to truly see her. She felt for the first time visible to someone, who seemed genuinely interested in understanding her. For the first time, she began to share some of what it had been like with Andrew to grow up with a mentally ill father and he seemed to really get it. He seemed to possess none of the emotional volatility of her father. She trusted his integrity, and saw him as steady and confident.

When she first began to sense him getting wounded and shutting down, she was at a loss to understand what was happening. It not only did not make sense to her, but it also frightened her. It brought back powerful memories of her father's moodiness, which was often the sign of something dangerous to come. Therefore, in response she did what she always did as a child when her father would seem emotional—she shut down as a defense against creating more problems and stirring things up more. Unfortunately, as she shut down, Andrew felt even more alone, and misunderstood, which created more distance between them. As these cycles of distance continued to get worse, the couple became more and more emotionally distant. Both began to question whether this was a marriage that would work for the long term. Andrew began to feel just as misunderstood as he did as a child, and Kim began to feel the same tension that she had felt as a child. Neither knew what to do.

To find the "salvation" and wholeness that they craved much work was going to be necessary. Both came from difficult childhoods, but longed for something different, and both thought they had found it in the early stages of their relationship.

STEPS TO WHOLENESS AND SALVATION: PROVIDENCE

For this couple, and most couples for that matter, to find what they are looking for is to enter into the spiritual work of marriage described throughout the earlier chapters in this book.

This spiritual work begins with an assumption—one that is difficult to hold onto when things get difficult. This assumption is that the person you married is the person you should have married and can be your greatest asset to help you on a spiritual path. You *have* found the ideal partner. In some religious traditions, this is called providence. Providence, talked about by Calvin, but broadened by other thinkers refers to a general belief about God's benevolent attention to what people need, and that on some level God is looking ahead to what people need. Out of that belief emerges trust that our life experiences, and life partner, are exactly what we need in order to grow spiritually. The notion of providence suggests that if one believes that God is attentive to human needs and looks ahead to what they need then trust can emerge.

Some would argue that this sounds like naïve thinking. Yet is this not on some level what is being implied during a marriage ceremony? Is there not some partial assumption that we have found the "perfect" partner, and that God is somehow involved in that selection? Implied in the religious part of the ceremony is that somehow this is God's plan, and therefore it is a plan for life. If couples can recognize providence and rejoice in the fact that they have found the "ideal" partner to travel a spiritual path with, as well as keeping in mind the challenges they will face with each other and with themselves, there is less chance for disillusionment.

In reality, many couples therapists believe in providence in a nonreligious or nonspiritual way. It is striking to me after many years of providing couples therapy, how often people have actually found what they need. Often they are not conscious of this, often they forget it, and sometimes they cannot make it work. However, none of that changes the fact that much of the time couples did know what they were doing. The introvert married the extrovert hoping to find balance and the extrovert married the introvert hoping for grounding. The overresponsible person marries the fun, relaxed person looking for help in slowing down and the relaxed person marries looking for more security. The woman with a domineering father who never won his approval marries a man who is also domineering, hoping for redemption—hoping to rework old material. The domineering man finds "salvation" as his wife defines herself nonreactively and does not allow him to dominate her, winning his respect, and a softening of this soul. The examples can be numerous, but they suggest that somehow providence is at work. Psychoanalytic theorists talk about providence from the vantage point that couples marry to work out old issues, while the late family therapist Murray Bowen (Bowen and Kerr, 1988) suggests that a person always marries someone who is at the same level of differentiation from their family of origin. Even if they may express this very differently, such as one partner overfunctioning and doing all the work around the house while the other plays around, one partner is not more mature or differentiated than the other. In his book *Should You Leave?*, Peter Kramer (1999) summarizes this notion as follows: "Where you are is probably not far from where you ought to be. This is the principle of matched differentiation, ... Whom you have chosen speaks to who you are" (p. 128). This notion suggests that people choose what they need in a way that connects with who they are. All of this is to illustrate that providence is part of marital selection, and that the acceptance of that can help create trust.

The notion of providence, or "matched differentiation" (Kramer, 1999) can provide optimism in the face of discouragement and sometimes despair. Too often people express their hopelessness in statements such as "Why do I always pick the same person? When will I ever learn?" This can leave people feeling hopeless and believing that they have made a huge mistake. Providence suggests that there is work to be done and that part of a spiritual journey is working things out with the person you have "chosen." Providence says they are essential to your spiritual journey.

This was certainly true for Andrew and Kim. As their marriage bogged down in the predictable stage of disillusionment, remembering that there was a reason for choosing each other was helpful. This belief in providence, or Bowen's notion that people marry someone at the same level of differentiation, can help enhance trust. Acceptance that there was a reason for marital selection, and trusting that there was some reason for that selection, can provide not only trust but also hope. This hope is important, and can give people motivation to work on their marriage. Statistically, second marriages fail more than the first, so it can be in one's best interest to work through the challenges of marriage, rather than getting divorced.

Andrew and Kim needed to remember what drew them together. It is always interesting as a couples therapist to ask couples how their relationship began and what attracted them to each other. Usually there is warmth, laughter, and smiles as they remember. Couples quickly forget the good stuff when disillusionment hits.

LOCK THE DOORS

Understanding the spiritual concept of providence, and the notion that couples do actually choose for a reason, suggests another principle that will help them find satisfaction and even salvation. That is, during the times of disillusionment, which are part of every relationship, it is important to "lock the exit doors" of the relationship. I frequently ask couples that I am working with to rule out the option of separation during the intense work of couples therapy since even talking about separation interferes with rebuilding trust and intimacy. Along the same lines, fidelity is a necessary commitment. During stages of disillusionment, it will be easy for Kim and Andrew to meet others who they mistakenly think would be a better match. The temptation for an "affair" is significant during these difficult times, even though the result of such affairs is usually a disaster for everyone involved. Fidelity is one more element of a spiritual practice. Part of the idea of a covenant, introduced in the Old Testament, to describe God's relationship with Israel, is the expectation of fidelity to the covenant.

For Kim and Andrew, as well as for all couples, the spiritual work of marriage is to build on a foundation of providence, and fidelity to the covenant of marriage and to each other. This beginning practice is a necessary foundation on which the rest of the spiritual work of marriage is built. For Kim and Andrew, remembering their history, reflecting on what drew them together and what they were initially attracted to will be something to return to. Some philosophers remind us that language can create reality. This is if we are constantly talking about what is wrong, then all we can see is what is wrong. If we remember what is good, and what drew us together, it is much easier to create positive energy.

BEING KNOWN, EMPATHIC ATTUNEMENT, AND INCARNATION

For Andrew and Kim to move forward in their quest for wholeness, they will need to stay focused on the ongoing work of really knowing each other. If they accept that there is something providential about their life together then it is essential that they continue attempt to know each other more deeply as was described in Chapter 2. Both will have some significant work to do. Andrew will need to realize that when he gets wounded and shuts down, he is blocking Kim from knowing him more deeply. When he gets hurt, he will need to struggle to find words to express what he is feeling. If he feels misunderstood, then he will need to explain to Kim whenever he does not feel misunderstood and try to keep the conversations going until some increased understanding is possible. Too often when feeling misunderstood, we like Andrew, begin a process of internal dialogue that becomes angry and critical. That internal dialogue will always make things worse.

"She is just choosing to not understand right now, and is ignoring me. I cannot believe I married such a cold wife. I'm sure she listens to her friends. . . ." Or "He would much rather watch football than understand that I'm hurting. I married such an immature man—he would much rather drink beer and watch football with his friends. And he wonders why I'm not interested in sex. . . ."

Andrew and Kim must recognize the dangers of this type of internal dialogue. Andrew, when he feels hurt and misunderstood must find words to describe what he is feeling. Kim must be equally careful when she feels that Andrew is shutting down to not carry on her own internal dialogue. It is too easy for her to begin to see Andrew as being like her father, and then want distance. She will need to work on her ability to hold onto herself and stay connected when Andrew is shutting down, as opposed to distancing. It is necessary for her to recognize this tendency and work on better understanding what is happening between them.

Knowing each other deeply means recognizing what happens when they get hurt or anxious. Both fall back on old, familiar patterns. Andrew shuts down and gets wounded when he feels misunderstood, and Kim distances. These are patterned defenses that both learned as children. In times of great anxiety, we tend to fall back on more primitive defense mechanisms. These defenses then block deep knowing and deep connecting.

This couple had prided themselves on understanding each other at the beginning of their relationship. However, maintaining that level of understanding during the complexity of life together with busy schedules and conflicting needs is far from easy, especially when old defenses get activated. They will need to learn more about each other's childhoods and more about how each learned to cope. What is important is not more detail about their childhoods, but more of how each coped with their respective families and how that is interfering with deep knowing in the present.

Their goal is not to change the other, but to practice acceptance. While it is one thing to say that the only person we can ever change is our self, it is another to put that into practice.

The spiritual work in this is not simply knowing one's partner, but offering acceptance or what in spiritual language is called grace. What most people crave in the depths of their being is being known and feeling accepted even in the midst of their imperfections. Grace speaks to God's unconditional acceptance. Grace speaks to the radical fact that there is nothing we can do to earn God's favor—we are simply accepted. The stories in the gospel illustrate this. Jesus did not offer acceptance after people changed their lives. It was not contingent on what they did or how they lived. Rather, he offered radical acceptance to all, even those considered outcasts, in the midst of their brokenness. Any change followed grace. St. Paul summarized it by saying "For by Grace are you saved. . . ."

For couples, there is an opportunity to do profound spiritual work. It is the work of mediating God's grace and acceptance to one's partner. The goal of deep knowing and empathic attunement is not just to know one's partner more deeply. Rather it is to know and to accept and offer grace. This is the long-term work of marriage. To be fully known as imperfect and flawed but to be accepted in the midst of that imperfection is liberating. It points beyond itself to the acceptance of God. To be known and loved and accepted points to the grace offered by God. Perhaps it is not surprising that in the midst of sexual passion one might exclaim "Oh God." In that moment of fusion, union, and being known, perhaps something transcendent is also happening.

BLOCKS TO BEING KNOWN

Unfortunately this work of being known and offering acceptance runs into roadblocks. These have been described in detail in Chapter 3. The opposite of empathic attunement and grace is the attempt to change one's partner, or what has been referred to as idolatry. As summarized in Chapter 3, idolatry is the way in which we try to turn our partner into what we think we need. The more anxious we become the more we try to create this change. The more we try to change our partner the more conflicted the relationship becomes.

Kim used to describe Andrew to her friends as wonderful, deeply caring, and solid. She could not find enough positive words to describe him. Andrew, in the early stage, wanted nothing more than to be with Kim and to get to know her more and more deeply.

As time went on, and irritants and disillusionment set it, they began to be more frustrated with each other, and slowly began to try to change the other. Kim began to push Andrew to be more extroverted and to have more friends. She wished he would not get wounded so easily and wished he would just bounce back. In frustration she yelled, "Can't you just lighten up—does everything have to be so intense all of the time." Andrew frequently accused Kim of being insensitive and uncaring. He blurted out, "You don't even know what empathy is." He wished she could understand him more deeply, connect more emotionally, and spend less time with her friends. The more he pushed her the more emotionally distant she became. At times his pressure made her so anxious that she found if difficult to respond.

Their goal is certainly to work at knowing the other, but attempts to change the other make this impossible. They need to remember that the spiritual work of knowing is built on several principles:

- The only person you can change is you.
- Therefore, the only thing you can work on is your own differentiation. In other words, work on your own growth, your own ability to hold onto yourself nonreactively, and your own capacity to listen.
- Then let go of trying to change and practice acceptance by focusing on deep knowing and understanding.

This, of course, is the work of a lifetime. It is the work of long-term marriage. It is the spiritual work of marriage that provides grace, which leads to salvation and wholeness.

REDEMPTION AND GRACE

Andrew and Kim also illustrate the longings that are brought to marriage. They both experienced difficult childhoods and formed adaptive ways of coping with the families they grew up in. Despite their success, they hoped and unconsciously longed for something "redemptive" from their partner. Andrew longed to be understood and accepted in a way that he had never experienced. He craved mirroring and validation, and being known and not judged, but he married a woman who tended to distance. The more she distanced the more hurt he became. Kim also wanted to be known and hoped that Andrew would be solid and steady. Unfortunately, when he would withdraw and get wounded she concluded that she would not be understood.

Both longed for redemption and grace and both were concluding that they were not going to find it with their partner. As Chapter 4 illustrated they needed to work on removing the blocks that would lead to redemption. Both longed to be released from their childhood roles, not to mention liberated from their childhood rules. Andrew wanted an accepting environment, and Kim wanted to not always be hypervigilant. Certainly both wanted healing from their childhood injuries.

Getting there was the problem. For redemption to occur, the blocks of poor communication, assumptions, and internal dialogue must all be removed. Belief systems that block one from seeing one's partner must also be removed, and unconscious longing must be made conscious. It is one thing for Kim to understand the powerful dysfunctions of Andrew's family; it is quite another to understand just how much Andrew longed to be seen and understood. In a similar way, it is one thing for Andrew to understand the fear Kim experienced having a mentally ill father who could blow up at any time. It is quite another to understand how hypervigilant Kim had become and how she automatically distanced when things got emotional. While, Andrew was at times irritated by Kim's extroverted style, he needed to understand how that style had "saved" her during her childhood.

For redemption to occur, both would have to stop changing the other or being critical of the other's style. What is required is deep understanding, not just of their respective histories, but of how each formed defensive and adaptive ways of responding. They cannot heal each other or make up for what was missing in each other's childhood. However, by deep understanding, empathic attunement, and the offering of acceptance and grace, redemption can move forward.

Redemption is difficult work. Attempts to change each other, counterproductive belief systems, faulty communication, and pictures that are formed of one's partner all block redemption. Yet in the working through of these blocks by deep empathy and acceptance redemption is possible.

Repentance

Unfortunately, on the road to redemption and deep understanding, damage is done. After working with hundreds of couples, I believe that for the most part couples are doing the best they can. They do not mean to hurt each other, and typically are doing their best.

Yet the reality of marriage is that couples do hurt each other without meaning to. Andrew and Kim, like most couples planned on a wonderful life together. The plan did not include hurting each other. Yet like all of us, they ended up hurting each other in multiple ways. Kim never meant to misunderstand Andrew and certainly did not want him to feel misunderstood. Certainly Andrew never meant to punish Kim with his shutting down and with his fears of her going out. Both wanted to be understanding of what the other needed and certainly meant to be loving. They both had the best of intentions. Yet the reality of their relationship was that in the end they did hurt each other in a variety of ways. For them, and for all couples, repentance is an essential spiritual practice. It is useless to focus on the sins of the other. What is helpful is to practice the spiritual discipline of repentance. This involves not focusing on trying to change the other, but focusing on how our actions are often hurtful and contribute to misunderstanding. Repentance is taking responsibility to "confess" the ways we have not been understanding, empathically attune, as well as taking the responsibility to make the deep change necessary for that change to occur. Repentance is a necessary part of helping one's partner find salvation and wholeness.

Forgiveness

Finally, as repentance is practiced as a spiritual discipline, then it must be met with forgiveness. The reality of attempting to build marital intimacy, build deep understanding, and redemption en route to helping each other find salvation and wholeness is that there will be hurt and misunderstanding along the way. Self-awareness that leads to repentance is an essential ingredient for both marriage and developing spiritual maturity. However, forgiveness must be present along with repentance for real healing to occur.

Andrew and Kim will come to realize on their journey to salvation and wholeness that they have misunderstood each other in numerous ways and without meaning to hurt each other. As each comes to grip with this reality, repentance will be an important step. Forgiveness is a response to that level of repentance. While certainly forgiveness is a complicated spiritual exercise as described in Chapter 6, yet, without forgiveness there will be no wholeness or intimacy. Repentance without forgiveness can lead to reinforcement of negative patterns or of one partner talking all the blame. Forgiveness when coupled with repentance can be transformational.

STEPS TO SALVATION AND WHOLENESS

Andrew and Kim illustrate the longing for salvation, redemption, and wholeness. Their struggle is in the end a struggle to find grace and deep acceptance; an acceptance that points beyond itself to something transcendent. In the end the journey of marriage is a journey to find deep empathic connection, deep healing, but finally deep acceptance and grace. There are steps to be followed in the quest. Marriage as spiritual work involves several steps that have been outlined in this book. They are as follows:

- Choose to see marriage as a covenant rich with spiritual opportunity. It is in the end an opportunity to work out spiritual issues in a relational context.
- Remember the notion of providence and how it intersects with Bowen's notion that you have found what you need. As you close the exits, you practice the spiritual discipline of covenant faithfulness.
- Work on empathic understanding, remembering Steven Covey's suggestion to first try to understand as opposed to being understood. Focus on knowing your spouse deeply and finding ways to more fully enter their subjective experience.
- Recognize that the only person you can change is you. You can never change your partner and the attempt to do so is idolatry. Rather focus on your own work on differentiation and continue to do the spiritual work of attempting to understand your partner.
- Recognize the longing for redemption. Part of getting to know one's partner more deeply is to understand what your partner is longing to have redeemed. It also involves being conscious about your own longings for redemption.

- Finally, recognize the need for repentance and forgiveness as an ongoing part of the work of marriage.
- You have found the "ideal" partner. Following these steps, marriage can become a spiritual journey that can bring both individual and relational transformation.

References

Bowen, M. and Kerr, M.E. (1988). *Family Evaluation: An Approach Based on Bowen Theory.* New York: W.W. Norton & Company.

Brown, C. (Ed.) (1971). *The New International Dictionary of New Testament Theology,* Volume 3. Grand Rapids, MI: The Zondervan Corporation.

Buber, M. (1996). *I and Thou.* New York: Touchstone.

Fleischman, P.R. (1990). *The Healing Spirit: Explorations in Religion and Psychotherapy.* New York: Paragon House.

Hendrix, H. (1988). *Getting the Love You Want: A Guide for Couples.* New York: Henry Holt and Company.

Kierkegaard, S. (1983). *The Sickness unto Death: A Christian Psychological Exposition for Upbuilding and Awakening.* Princeton, NJ: Princeton University Press.

Kohut, H. (1984). *How Does Analysis Cure?* Chicago: University of Chicago Press.

Kramer, P.D. (1999). *Should You Leave? A Psychiatrist Explores Intimacy and Autonomy—and the Nature of Advice.* New York: Penguin Books.

Norris, K. (1998). *Amazing Grace: A Vocabulary of Faith.* New York: Riverhead Books.

Olsen, D.C. and Stephens, D. (2001). *The Couple's Survival Workbook.* Oakland, CA: New Harbinger Publications.

Peck, S.M. (2003). *The Road Less Traveled: A New Psychology of Love, Traditional Values and Spiritual Growth,* 25th anniversary edition. New York: Touchstone.

Schnarch, D. (1997). *Passionate Marriage: Love, Sex, and Intimacy in Emotionally Committed Relationships.* New York: W.W. Norton & Company.

Tillich, P. (1951). *Existence and the Christ: Systematic Theology.* Chicago: University of Chicago Press.

Tillich, P. (2000). *The Courage to Be.* New Haven, CT: Yale University Press.

Walsh, F. (2003). *Spiritual Resources in Family Therapy.* New York: Guilford Press.

www.smartmarriages.com/remarrying.html.

Index

A

Advice, 49
    as roadblock to empathetic
        understanding, 21
Anxiety, 5, 17, 22, 28, 35, 47, 80
    biblical perspectives, 38
    childhood, 42
    chronic, 44
    existential, 7
    of vulnerability, 70
    primitive defense mechanisms and, 88
    role of religion in calming, 6
    separation, 30

B

Being known, 87–89
    anxiety and, 5
    as spiritual goal, 12–13
    blocks to, 89–90
    incarnation and, 13–15
    longing to be, 11–23
Belief, power of, 15–16

C

Childhood
    anxiety, 42
    wounds, redemption from, 44–48
Christianity
    concept of sin in, 80
    knowing and, 13
    language of, 7
    traditions in, 4, 5, 7

D

Dances
    blocking acceptance and grace,
        33–35

Dances (*continued*)
    hopeless, 31–35
    negative effects, 33–35
    over-under responsible pattern,
        32–33
    pursuer-distancer, 31–32
Differentiation, 47
    as lifelong journey, 47
    capacity for, repentance and,
        63, 77
    defined, 63
    from family of origin, 85
    from parents, 37
    level of, 63
        communication and, 76
    matched, 85, 86
    work of, 76

E

Empathic attunement, 47
    defined, 12
    earlier steps in, 46
    factors that interfere with, 15
    goal of, 89
    opposite of, 89
    roadblocks on journey to, 21–22
    search for, 16
    ultimate exercise in, 14

F

False self, 81
Family
    of origin, 38–48
        differentiation from, 85
        map of, 39–41
        redemption from childhood
            wounds from, 44–48

Family (*continued*)
   redemption from painful
      experiences in, 38–39
   rituals of, 41–42
   roles and scripts for, 42–44
  power of, 38–39
Fix-it people, as roadblock to
   empathetic understanding, 21
Forgiveness, 7, 62, 65–77, 92–93
  application to, 66
  as leap of faith, 69–70
  biblical accounts of, 65–66
  canceling debt in, 72–74
  complexity of, 66, 69
  confrontation and, 71–72
  genuine, 76
  intimacy and, 74–77
  origin of, 66
  power and, 70
  repentance and, 49
  request for, 63
  risks associated, 69
  start of, 66
  steps of, 70–77
    summary of, 77

H
Hopeless dances, 31–35

I
Idealization, 19–20
Idolatry
  biblical, 29–31
  changing your partner as form of, 35
  intimacy and, 31
Incarnation, 13–15
Intimacy
  forgiveness and, 74–77
  idolatry and, 31
  spiritual, 6

L
Loneliness, 11
Longing for twinship, 18

M
Marriage
  as a type of salvation, 80

Marriage (*continued*)
  as spiritual work, 3–4, 8
   impedients to, 16
  beliefs about, 16–19
  dream, 1–2
  failed, 3
  fantasies, 79
  longing for connectedness and, 80
  of Adam and Eve, 4
  reality, 2–4
  redemption from childhood wounds
   in, 44–48
   action steps, 47–48
   goal of, 45–47
  spirituality and, 6–7
  vows, 2

P
Perfection, elusive search for, 28–29
Premarital counseling, 1
Providence, 86

R
Redemption
  beginnings of, 46
  from childhood wounds, 44–45
  goal in marriage, 45
  grace and, 90–93
  longing for, 41, 42
  spiritual work of, 46
  steps necessary for, 47
  transformation and, 46
  work of, 46
Relationship rule, 26–28
Religion
  function, 5
  spirituality *vs.,* 4–5
  traditions and, 5
Repentance, 49–55, 62–63, 91–92
  action steps toward, 62–63
  genuine, 63
  importance of, 50–52
  projection and, 52–54
  skills as part of, 54–55

S
Salvation
  marriage and, 80, 82–84
  religious concept, 80–82